Seven Myths of Youth Ministry

Seven Myths of Youth Ministry

How to re-ignite your passion

Nigel James
with Gary Smith

Authentic

10 09 08 07 06 05 04   7 6 5 4 3 2 1

First published 2004 by Authentic Media
9 Holdom Avenue, Bletchley, Milton Keynes, Bucks, MK1 1QR, UK
and PO Box 1047, Waynesboro, GA 30830-2047, USA.
www.authenticmedia.co.uk

British Library Cataloguing in Publication Data.
A catalogue record for this book is available from the British Library.

ISBN 1-85078-574-0

Cover design by Jeremy Bye
Typeset by Temple Design
Print Management by Adare Carwin
Printed and bound by AIT Nørhaven A/S, Denmark

CONTENTS

FOREWORD

As we go through life we all rely so much on the skills of others. They may be plumbers, brain surgeons or double-glazing salespeople. If you are fortunate, then sometime before you really need them, you will meet somebody who knows the best plumber, most skilful brain-surgeon and somebody who installs windows that really will keep out the elements! When you eventually meet these characters you may find that in technical ability they are a little ahead of the competition, but that's not what really sets them apart. They have what I call 'Factor X.' It is that rare ability that allows them to feel the job they do – to really understand the customer, to guess at his or her fears, and to convince that person, 'you can trust me.'

When it comes to working with young people Gary and Nigel have 'Factor X.' In fact they have it in such abundance it is awesome to watch. These guys are not in their twenties, and although it may disappoint them to read it, young people don't respond to them because they look like members of a boy band. No, these men have decades of experience in youth work; they understand young people, and I believe with all my heart that they love young people. And those simple qualities mean they love what they do. They are people we can learn from.

I wonder what qualities it takes to be really effective in working with young people. One youth worker put it like this:

First you need a love for God, and next a love for young people – a love that will survive when they let you down, abuse you and help to smash your dreams for the amazing programme you have devised for them. And when they have done all that to you and then turn up one day at the door of the church as if nothing has happened, you will need to be able to take them in and start again.

Nigel and Gary have not only done just this hundreds of times, they have taught thousands of people how to do it – not least by their example.

I commend Nigel and Gary to you and I commend their book. If you've got an ounce of 'Factor X' in youth work, *Seven Myths of Youth Ministry* will help you use it effectively. I hope you enjoy it.

Rob Parsons

INTRODUCTION

Melting the myths

Someone once said 'never let the facts get in the way of a good story' – it might have been a journalist or an evangelist – and that is certainly the case with myths. A myth can be a legend, part of folklore, or simply a traditional tale; but one thing is certain: although perhaps based on an initial truth, or having a grain of truth somewhere in them, myths are essentially fictional. Over recent years we have had the rise of urban myths – stories that we hear happened to a friend of a friend or that a friend heard from someone else – so it must be true! Recent myths that I've come across include the following:

- *NASA scientists have discovered a lost day in time.*
- *Police have uncovered a plot to throw out the Royal family and replace them with David and Victoria Beckham.*
- *Scientists drilling in Siberia broke through into hell.*
- *A well-known fast food chain is the world's largest purchaser of cow eyeballs.*
- *Stephen Spielberg got his start in the film industry by wandering into Universal Studios and taking over an unoccupied office.*

All complete fabrications, and you could name many more that have arrived in your inbox or been told to you by the friend of a friend. Disturbingly, some spiritual urban myths end up in the sermons of pastors and preachers, but I guess that needs to be dealt with in another book. This one is concerned with melting some of the myths that surround youth ministry; they may have started from an inkling of truth, they may have good intentions, but they have infiltrated youth ministry to the extent that many of us now take as gospel truth phrases and clichés that owe more to legend and tradition than they do to biblical precedent or present day good practice. Some of these myths you will easily see through; others you may have fallen for at some stage. One or two you might initially agree with and wouldn't say were a myth at all.

Each of the seven chapters focuses on one myth in particular, and starts with a 'rant' from my good friend and colleague, Gary Smith. He has been co-director of Big Ideas and Ignite alongside me for the nine years of our ministry. During that time Gary has consistently acted as a supervisor to many youth ministry students who were studying with the YMCA or the Centre for Youth Ministry in Bristol. To get our spiritual temperature going and to help our passion rise, I've asked Gary to give us his 'no holds barred' assessment of why the particular myth in the chapter can be so damaging.

During the last few months Gary and I have been travelling to various towns and cities around the UK talking to groups of youth leaders about our Ignite initiative and we've taken the liberty of melting the myths with them. As a result, you'll also find in each chapter a quote or two from 'a youth leader' – these are all real quotes from real youth leaders.

If you were in one of our meetings in Torquay, Hitchin, Bristol, Congleton, Norwich, Glasgow, Cardiff, with the SWYM staff, or with the Crusaders staff – then thank you! You might recognise your own words.

To whet your appetite for the rest of the book we are going to kick things off by examining three myths that don't warrant a chapter each but do help us establish the ground we are covering, and more importantly the truth we hold to.

1. It's not ministry

In the UK I'm afraid, I still stumble across churches that are playing games at youth ministry. Some give the job of youth ministry to someone by default, often a parent, or the youngest and most inexperienced member of staff. Some persist with what I call 'the tuck shop and table tennis model' – relying on a ping-pong table and a few cold drinks to keep young people occupied for an evening. The scene in the United States is better, but even there by comparison to other areas of ministry youth work is not treated seriously.

Even in the bigger churches on both sides of the Atlantic, youth work is occasionally seen as a 'holding job' until young people become adults and join in the adult life of the church.

I much prefer to use the term 'ministry' for the work that churches undertake with young people because it is exactly that. Youth ministry, as this book should confirm to you, is so much more than just keeping them off the streets. In fact you can call it what you like but it is a vital and valuable ministry in the church of Jesus, and should be treated seriously. Youth ministry deserves commitment and any notion of half-heartedness needs to be banished.

We read these words of Jesus in Revelation to the church at Laodicea: 'I know your deeds, that you are neither cold nor hot. I wish you were either one or the other! So, because you are lukewarm – neither hot nor cold – I am about to spit you out of my mouth' (Rev. 3:15-16).

Their lack of enthusiasm and passion, their complacency and indifference to the Christian life of discipleship was so disgusting to Jesus that it made him sick. Wholehearted, passionate followers are what Jesus wants.

Throughout his letters Paul constantly explains the motivation for his ministry. In Galatians he recognises that the same God who worked through Peter's ministry to the Jews worked through his own ministry to the Gentiles. In 2 Corinthians he gives this powerful description of ministry

> *He has made us competent as ministers of a new covenant – not of the letter but of the Spirit; for the letter kills, but the Spirit gives life. Now if the ministry that brought death, which was engraved in letters on stone, came with glory, so that the Israelites could not look steadily at the face of Moses because of its glory, fading though it was, will not the ministry of the Spirit be even more glorious? If the ministry that condemns men is glorious, how much more glorious is the ministry that brings righteousness! For what was glorious has no glory now in comparison with the surpassing glory (2 Cor. 3:6-10).*

Other translations of this passage help us to realise that ministry really means being 'representatives' of Jesus and of the new covenant, bringing life instead of death to people. In fact, *The Message* tells us that 'God….authorizes us to help with this new plan of action', and the passage above confirms to us that being involved in this ministry is 'glorious'. A few chapters later in the same letter we read that: 'All this is from God, who reconciled us to himself through Christ and gave us the ministry of reconciliation' (2 Cor. 5:18).

Another way of looking at ministry is to say that every Christian has been given the task of bringing people back to God. Isn't that exactly what youth ministry should be about?

However, a word of warning. In the book of Acts we can see the dangers of being wrongly motivated for ministry. A man called Simon the Sorcerer witnessed the apostles laying hands on people so that they would receive the Holy Spirit. Simon offered the apostles money in order to obtain the same gifting. Peter answered him: 'You have no part or share in this ministry, because your heart is not right before God' (Acts 8:21).

Your main motivation for working with young people should be a belief that God has called you to a vital ministry and you should consider yourself a minister of the gospel. We'll look a bit more at what that means in Myth Four.

2. Young people aren't interested in Christianity

When Christianity was part of our culture and its beliefs were handed down in homes and schools, its familiarity kept strong. Everyone knew Bible stories, hymns and prayers. Now it is at least as alien to many young people as Islam, if not more so because it does not seem to be interested in them.

Peter Hitchens, *The Mail on Sunday*, November 2nd 2003

These days it's not so much that young people haven't heard the gospel, it's that they think they know what Christianity is, and they've decided they don't want any.

Steve Taylor, 'Are You a Minister or an Entertainer?'
Youthspecialties.com, December 2002

The opinion that young people are no longer interested in Christianity is a commonly held one. Peter Hitchens comments on the widening gulf between Christianity and young people, and even the respected Christian singer, writer and spokesman Steve Taylor concedes that we have a real challenge to get the attention of a generation who don't want to listen. I'm not sure that either of them has accurately reflected the real truth. I readily agree that we now live in a post-Christian or even anti-Christian culture, and that in many ways we exemplify the words of Paul to Timothy: 'For a time is coming when people will no longer listen to right teaching. They will follow their own desires and will look for teachers who will tell them whatever they want to hear. They will reject the truth and follow strange myths' (2 Tim. 4:3-4, NLT).

Paul's essentially warning Timothy about the possibility of error creeping into the early church, but he could just as easily be warning twenty-first century leaders about the challenge we face.

But despite all that, I do believe that young people are still interested in Christianity, or more accurately, fascinated by Jesus: both who he is and what he promised.

If we were to gather a group of leaders from ministries such as Soul Survivor, Youth for Christ, YWAM and OM, they would tell us that thousands and thousands of teenagers around the world are still being attracted to Jesus Christ. In the ministry of Ignite, we regularly work in high school religious education lessons where words like 'church', 'religion,' and 'Christians' are met with scepticism and cynicism. However, the actual life of Jesus, and particularly the story of the cross, is invariably met with a healthy dose of genuine questions. Often I ask pupils a question myself: 'If there is a God and you could live with him forever, how many of you would be interested in checking it out?' The response is always a majority in favour of exploring eternal life.

There is undoubtedly a spiritual hunger amongst young people in the twenty-first century, the likes of which hasn't been seen or experienced by their parents.

Understand how we think and how we feel. Reach out to us on our own terms. Like Jesus, put yourself in our reality and see the world through our eyes and feel the world through our feelings. Then you will have something authentic to say to us. Then we will listen.

Kevin Ford, *Jesus for a New Generation*[i]

So it's clear that if we show genuine and relevant interest and concern for young people they will be ready to begin the journey of discovering and following Jesus. The challenge is not to undervalue the commitment of a young person, but to actively demonstrate our own.

3. We've always done it like that

The world is full of people whose notion of a satisfactory future is, in fact, a return to an idealized past.

Robertson Davies quoted by Leonard Sweet in *Soul Tsunami*[ii]

Jesus is eating dinner on one occasion when the disciples of John the Baptist approach him and criticise the behaviour of his own disciples. Jesus replies to them with these memorable words

No one sews a patch of unshrunk cloth on an old garment, for the patch will pull away from the garment, making the tear worse. Neither do men pour new wine into old wineskins. If they do, the skins will burst, the wine will run out and the wineskins will be ruined. No, they pour new wine into new wineskins, and both are preserved (Mt. 9:16-17).

Jesus is saying that the totally new situation he brings with him can't simply be patched onto the old traditions of Judaism, nor could it be poured into the old wineskin of Judaism.

The implication of this illustration has been an important one for the church throughout the centuries, and there have been seasons when God has called for new garments, new wine and new wineskins. The application to youth ministry is that many traditional and established methods of working need to be laid aside for a new paradigm.

If we weren't doing this today, would we start doing it now?

Peter Drucker quoted by Leonard Sweet in *Soul Tsunami*

There is a phrase in media circles called 'W-3' or 'W-cubed'. It stands for: Whatever, Whenever, Wherever it takes to get the job done. For us that means we have to take seriously the challenge of doing whatever it takes, going wherever it takes, and working whenever it takes to fruitfully evangelise and disciple young people in the twenty-first century. Our content is always the good news of Jesus, and that is unchanging, but the container that we use has to be a contemporary one.

Three myths that you didn't really need melting because you probably didn't believe any of them in the first place. But they have served as a good starter for the main course of the book. We'll be looking at seven myths – some of them will surprise you, some might make you angry, but most of all I pray that they will all encourage you to look deeply into your work with young people, and that they will stimulate you to build all you do on a God-given, thought-through foundation. We've taken the liberty of finishing each chapter with a 'reality check' of a few questions that will help you think things through from a personal perspective. Get ready to melt those myths!

Nigel James,
Cardiff,
December 2003

i Originally published in *Youthworker*, copyright 2004, Salem Publishing/CCM Communications. Reprinted with permission. For subscription information, visit www.youthworker.com

ii Kevin Ford, *Jesus for a New Generation*, (London: Hodder and Stoughton, 1996) p. 125.

iii Leonard Sweet, *Soul Tsunami*, (Grand Rapids: Zondervan, 2001).

MYTH 1

WE REALLY MAKE A DIFFERENCE IN OUR ONE HOUR A WEEK

When I was a teenager in church I went to the Boys' Brigade for three hours on a Friday night, a Bible class for an hour on a Sunday morning, as well as countless camps, trips, special events, concerts and other social activities. I look back now and think of the thirty or so young people who grew up with me in the church; as far as I know there are only two others who are still linked with a church in any way at all. You might say that three out of thirty, one in ten, ten per cent is not a bad return. But what about the nine out of ten? Despite the good efforts of our church to create a strong link that stretched to more than just the one hour a week, sooner or later ninety per cent of us were pulled in a direction that was stronger than the church youth group community. That's why it amazes me today that some churches still have the mentality that a one-hour-a-week programme is really going to be life-changing on its own for a generation of teenagers.

Community, intimacy, purpose

In Ignite we are constantly encouraging youth leaders to base their ministry on three principles – community, intimacy and purpose. These are powerfully modelled by Jesus' relationship with the disciples, and as always, he is our role model.

Young people need to belong before they believe, and that's why building up a community is so important. I initially went along to church to play football, go camping and learn to play a musical instrument. Those interests were great for enabling me to feel part of a community, but were not going to keep me part of a Christian community for my lifetime. Young people grow out of even the strongest youth group community and become attracted to the pull of conflicting activities. That's where intimacy with God comes in, and sadly the 'nine out of ten' never entered an intimate friendship with Jesus; for me it was different. I kept on as a part of the community and in time gave my life over to Jesus. Out of that intimacy comes an understanding of purpose in life and a desire to serve the kingdom. If young people aren't shown a kingdom purpose for their life then they will attempt to find purpose elsewhere and ultimately miss out on the very purpose for which they were created.

If you are as serious as us about community, intimacy and purpose, then you'll realize that the one hour a week of face-to-face meeting with young people must simply be the tip of the iceberg.

The best inheritance a parent can give to his children is a few minutes of their time each day.

Orlando A. Battista,
'The Speaker's Electronic Reference Collection', 1994

" Gary's Rant

One phrase I have heard a lot from youth workers when discussing their relationship with the young people in their group is: 'I am like a mother/father to them.' At such times I have often thought that if they truly believe this is the case then they are a lousy parent!

In recent years tabloid newspapers have recounted many stories about 'home alone kids': children who have effectively been left by parents to get on with life on their own. It seems to me that the youth workers I was referring to earlier are no different to the parents they are indirectly criticising. My point is a simple one. A crucial part of being a good parent is spending quality time with your kids. How would we judge a parent who only spent an hour or two each week with their children? Let's be honest. At best we would not be very impressed and at worst we would report them to social services. It's time for a reality check. If we want to develop significant and meaningful relationships we need to invest a very precious commodity: our time. For many young people, time is the one thing they do not receive from adults. In fact parents lavish 'things' on their children precisely because they are not able to commit face-to-face time.

Now you could argue that quality is more important than quantity. In many ways this is true but it is an unrealistic view of youth ministry. It suggests that when we are ready to do our work the young people should be ready to do their bit. Relationships are not like that! They are about mutual agreement and good timing. So some of our responsibility is to just be there. That will inevitably mean quantity as well as quality.

Many years ago, when I was working with a specific group of young people, I was going through a bit of a distracted patch and my programme planning was non-existent. In fact the only thing that I had going for me was that I turned up. It later became clear that merely turning up regularly was significant for two or three of the lads who I met each Monday because their fathers had recently left home. At that point they were not looking to be challenged, stretched or entertained; they were looking for security. I'm not trying to excuse my poor preparation but making the point that my commitment of time was a powerful tool in itself.

So those of us involved in youth ministry have to carve out that precious time, however costly it might sometimes be. Part of the calling will be to find out what we can give and then go the extra mile.

Time – what we are up against

If identity crisis is a form of madness, then young Britain 2002 is a schizoid manic depressive with bomb-site self-esteem. Our status as the most boozed up, drug-skewed, pregnancy prone wasters in Europe is pretty much unchallenged.

Mark Greene, Imagine Consultation, LICC 2003[i]

Just think for a moment about what consumes young people's time. School occupies about thirty hours a week – that's a big chunk. Are you aware of what is being taught in your local high school? Do you know current thinking in the curriculum regarding personal and social education, or religious education? Is there a CU meeting for pupils? Do you or anyone from your church ever visit the school? Discovery did some research in the West Midlands in the tail end of the 1990s and found that two-thirds of pupils named school as their main source of information about

Jesus.[ii] So do you know what schools are saying about Jesus?

A report issued by the Office for National Statistics in June 2000 noted that teenagers in the UK spent on average twelve hours a week watching television. We live in a rapidly changing world, and those figures would now be ranked alongside use of the computer, internet, instant messenger and text messaging on a mobile phone. The Reuters news information service issued a press release in July of 2003 stating that a recent report showed young people in the western world were now spending more time on the Web than watching TV. On average, young people said they spent nearly seventeen hours online each week, not including time used to read and send e-mail, compared with almost fourteen hours spent watching television and twelve hours listening to the radio.

Then we add into the mix the influence of family and peer group, both of which could be massive influences for good or bad, and we begin to see the competition we are up against to win the attention, the heart and the life of a young person. We shouldn't underestimate 'the power of the hour' – even one hour a week of contact with young people is better than no contact, and I believe that God is the God of the miraculous; he could break into the life of a young person in an instant. Yet if you and I want to be serious about helping bring a young generation to Jesus then we'll need to offer more than an hour a week programme.

A youth leader says:
'But don't underestimate the power of the hour!'

Jesus on time

Jesus varied his perspective on the amount of time he spent in his ministry. For three years he shared his everyday life with the disciples, and one day Philip asked Jesus to show him the Father. Jesus answered: 'Don't you know me, Philip, even after I have been among you such a long time? Anyone who has seen me has seen the Father. How can you say, "Show us the Father?"' (Jn. 14:9)

Jesus is reminding Philip and the rest of the disciples that Jesus himself is God incarnate. If we are serious about modelling ourselves on the life of Jesus then we'll want to live out his model, and seek to invest our lives into young people.

Yet on another occasion Jesus is questioned by the Pharisees about his authority and responds with the words: 'I am with you for only a short time, and then I go to the one who sent me' (Jn. 7:33).

So Jesus also recognized that in the light of eternity, his three years of ministry was a comparatively short period. Jesus spent thirty years in preparation for his ministry, but when he commenced the three years he never seemed to waste a moment of time. Youth ministry needs a lifestyle approach, but even then when you are working with young people the time is short. There will never be a better time to impact the life of an individual than when they are young.

A youth leader says:
'It has got to be about lifestyle not timetable.'

The apostle Paul on time

If you read through the book of Acts you will see that Paul was a man who knew what it meant to be sacrificial with his time. We know that throughout his missionary journeys he often spent part of his time as a tent-maker, so in today's terminology it would be debatable as to whether we said he was in full-time or part-time ministry. What can definitely be said is that he recognized that time commitment was important. Here are just some examples:

In Iconium: 'So Paul and Barnabas spent *considerable time* there, speaking boldly for the Lord, who confirmed the message of his grace by enabling them to do miraculous signs and wonders' (Acts 14:3, emphasis added).

Paul and Barnabas see incredible results as they hang out in the important Greek city of Iconium. Their investment bears fruit.

In Antioch: 'And when he found him, he brought him to Antioch. So for a *whole year* Barnabas and Saul met with the church and taught great numbers of people. The disciples were called Christians first at Antioch' (Acts 11:26, emphasis added).

The time commitment at Antioch even resulted in the very name that followers of Jesus have been called throughout the centuries.

'And they stayed there a *long time* with the disciples' (Acts 14:28, emphasis added).

After a missionary journey of about a year, Paul invests another whole year into the disciples in Antioch.

In Corinth: 'Paul stayed on in Corinth for *some time*' (Acts 18:18, emphasis added).

Scholars tell us that this 'some time' was almost certainly eighteen months or so of sustained preaching in the synagogue and the forum.

In Asia no time: 'Paul had decided to sail past Ephesus to *avoid spending time* in the province of Asia, for he was in a hurry to reach Jerusalem, if possible, by the day of Pentecost' (Acts 20:16, emphasis added).

Paul didn't want to visit Ephesus again on this trip because he had another priority in mind – Jerusalem. The boat Paul was on would have docked at Miletus for a few days and he took the opportunity to send a messenger to contact the leaders of the church in Ephesus to come and meet with him during his brief stay. He was able to remind the leaders of his character when he had been with them on a previous trip.

'From Miletus, Paul sent to Ephesus for the elders of the church. When they arrived, he said to them: "You know how I lived the *whole time* I was with you, from the first day I came into the province of Asia"' (Acts 20:17,18, emphasis added).

Paul didn't just focus on the face-to-face meetings with Christians, or a once weekly opportunity to preach to a crowd, he realized the importance of lifestyle and long-term investment into a group.

Half our life is spent trying to find something to do with the time we have rushed through life trying to save.

Will Rogers, www.motivational-inspirational-corner.com

Authenticity, availability, trust and transparency

I can well remember Carl, James and Adrian. I met them for the first time when they came to our church to join in the children's activities at the age of six. By the time they were eleven they had come into the youth group that I was leading as a volunteer, and I decided to spend as much time with them as possible. By the time they were teenagers (I was in my mid-twenties at the time) we went to concerts together, trips to the seaside, visits to the cinema; in fact despite the fact that I had a full-time job outside the church, lots of social stuff as well as the formal youth programme. The three of them were lively characters to say the least: immensely likeable but prone to get into trouble.

By the time they were all fifteen or so, it was me they would ring when they were in a mess; when caught graffiti-ing a school bus, violently sick at home after experimenting with drugs, facing shoplifting accusations. Even their parents recognized I could get through to them, or at least find out the truth, in a way no one else was able to do.

Now I'm not telling you this out of any sense of pride, just to illustrate that one of the strongest bonds I have ever had with a group of young people came out of deliberately giving them my time. The story of Carl, James and Adrian didn't even have a great ending really. All three of them made a commitment to Jesus at a Luis Palau crusade at QPR football stadium in London although later they admitted that a large incentive towards this act was that it meant they could go onto the pitch. At the time, QPR were renowned for having the first 'plastic' pitch in the land.

Eventually I moved on to a full-time job in Cardiff, the three guys left the church and I only heard of them sporadically through third parties. I often thought of them, and usually with regret. Some fifteen years after that I was on the road in the States with the band Newsboys when I got a phone call in my hotel room from my wife. James, now grown up with a wife and children, had been having an extremely tough time and had been near to breakdown point. In his moment of crisis, looking for someone to turn to he had attempted to track me down and had managed to get hold of my wife, Gill, on the phone. Once she had filled me in with the details, I rang James from America and spent ages in conversation with him, about his life, his family, his fears, his faith and old times. Towards the end of the conversation I asked him why he had to speak to me. He simply said that I'd always been prepared to give him time. I gave him a couple more hours of my time that night.

Never try to tell everything you know. It may take too short a time!

Norman Ford, www.quotationspage.com/quotes/Norman_Ford

Kevin Ford in his book *Jesus for a New Generation* suggests that time is one of the most important commodities we can invest in the life of a young person.[iii] He points out that to be effective in youth ministry into the twenty-first century we have to demonstrate authenticity, availability, trust and transparency. None of these can work without the added ingredient of time. To live authentic lives, to be available to young people, to be trusted, and to show transparency in our walk with God, will all take up our whole lives; not just our one or two hours worth of weekly programmes. We might be tempted into thinking this would be infinitely easier if we were employed full-time as youth leaders or ministers, but even when we are volunteers if our attitude is right, then there is ample opportunity to maximize our time wisely and to offer it to young people positively.

A youth leader says:
'If I can only give one hour a week to young people, I'm going to make sure it's the best hour.'

✔ REALITY CHECK

1. If you are a full-time youth minister how much time each week do you actually spend actually with young people?
2. If you are a volunteer youth leader how much more time than the 'one-hour-a-week' could you realistically give to young people?
3. What strategies could you develop to counteract the influences on the young people in your youth group outside the 'one-hour-a-week'?
4. When you have worked out how much time each week you can give to youth ministry, pray for wisdom from God to spend that time strategically.

Notes

i Originally quoted in *The Face* magazine.

ii Discovery is the school ministry of Agapé.

iii Kevin Ford, *Jesus for a New Generation* (London: Hodder & Stoughton, 1996).

MYTH 2

SIZE ISN'T IMPORTANT

This chapter is really about melting two myths in one go. We want to challenge the view that youth ministry is purely about quality and we want to challenge the view that youth ministry is simply about numbers. In fact we want to declare that youth ministry has to be about both, but should always be about growth.

I have some good friends called Russ and Lara Pawlowski who lead the Interface youth ministry at Heartland Church in Fort Wayne, Indiana. As I've observed them over the years they strike me as leaders who recognize that size *is* important. They see that BIG groups are important; they are always challenging their youth group to bring new people along, they are giving them opportunities to go to large-scale concerts and conferences, and want to see the numbers in their ministry grow. I travelled with them one Easter to a youth conference in Canada and there was a real buzz as their youth group crammed into a fifty-three-seater coach. There was an even bigger buzz at the conference, when the fifty or so from Heartland joined in with six thousand from all over Canada and the States. Yet Russ and Lara recognize the importance of small groups too, and have striven to provide every young person with an accountability group of one or two close friends. Russ himself puts time and effort into a handful of guys, whilst Lara does the same with a small group of girls.

The clear emphasis though is that they never want the whole youth ministry itself to be small. Now Russ and Lara aren't unique in their approach. Church growth experts for years have been telling us the importance of the cell (or small group), the congregation (or church) and the celebration (the big gathering), but whilst many youth leaders might agree with this they don't model it as a pattern for growth.

Gary's Rant

In the early nineties I went to visit a children's group that had nine children aged between the ages of eight and eleven. This was worthy of note because it represented nine out of the eleven children in this age range in the village. The other two children in the village were well-known to the leaders of the group, and had in fact been along on previous occasions.

My concern is not with this group in rural Norfolk but with the groups that have decided that small is beautiful; not out of a deliberate plan but rather as a result of their inability to attract or retain young people. Of course it is hardly surprising because many youth workers have been brought up in a church that has modelled this attitude for years. Declining numbers and waning interest have encouraged us all to make excuses as to why what we are doing is neither attractive nor engaging.

As a child I joined the Boys' Brigade. At the time the local group had lots of different ways to encourage other young people to join. Recruiting, as they called it, was always an important priority. As I grew up and became a leader in the group the tradition of 'recruitment drives' continued. Perhaps there is something to learn from that, and more importantly there is much to be learned from the first disciples and the earliest Christians. As Nigel showed in Myth 1, the early church often undertook mission trips in order to win people for Christ. In effect these were recruiting campaigns.

It is completely unacceptable to run a secret, exclusive club that outsiders can only join if they are brave enough to walk through the doors. My old Boys' Brigade company and the first apostles had a 'go' mentality that encouraged growth in an ordered and structured way.

One thing that is quite often intimidating for small growing youth groups is 'the large group in town.' To those of you who are intimidated by the success of others I would say don't be. Learn from it. What are they doing right? And how can you imitate or even emulate it? Often, however, a scratch beneath the surface might tell a different story. Many times when you investigate a large group you can observe that it is not growing but seeing a small and steady decline in numbers. Often the large ministry of today is heading towards being the small group of tomorrow.

When Nigel and I had been meeting with youth leaders recently in a variety of towns and cities, I asked: 'Who has got the biggest youth group in town?' Immediately everyone either mentions the name of a particular church or points to the youth leader from that church if they are present. At this point I tell them that there is a group that they have overlooked, a group that is much bigger, a group that is growing all the time and indeed some of the kids who used to be members of their church group have joined it.

The youth leaders scratch their heads, look puzzled and think furiously about which group they have overlooked; perhaps it's a new church they haven't heard of. Has the local authority begun to provide a massively successful youth centre they didn't know about? Then I reveal the answer. An answer I am confident is accurate in just about every village, town and city around the world. The Devil has the biggest youth group.

Getting deeper – Ignite

The main focus of all we do at Ignite is the Ignite Declaration (see Myth Five). Our aim has always been for as many young people as possible to sign and live out the life that the declaration sets out. At the time of writing there are just over two thousand five hundred young people who have signed the declaration and just over one thousand youth leaders around the UK in our network. We are still committed to pushing both figures up higher, but a while back we realized we shouldn't do that at the expense of deeper relationships with a smaller number. That's why Gary and I travelled around the UK for a couple of months on and off consulting youth leaders – some of whom are quoted in this book. Similarly, we recommitted ourselves to train, equip and release young people by means of our internship scheme and our newly established Ignite Leadership Academy. So as well as e-mailing the two thousand five hundred Ignite card-holders twice a month and the youth leaders once a month, we have up to four young people working with us in our ministry for a year at a time and we accept twelve students onto our academy twice a year.

We want as many young people as possible to be ignited with a passion for Jesus from all that we do, but we recognize the need to build deeply into the lives of a smaller number of young people that God brings our way. For us the balance between large size and small size is an important one and one that we always try to identify and address.

Size is important to Jesus

When we see the way Jesus built relationships with his followers, we see that groups of all different sizes fitted into his plan. Three times in John's gospel we read about 'the disciple whom Jesus loved' – John himself was singled out for that special relationship. Then we know that Jesus spent significant time with Peter, James and John: 'After six days Jesus took Peter, James and John with him and led them up a high mountain, where they were all alone. There he was transfigured before them' (Mk. 9:2).

So Jesus invested into his own small group of closest friends and he spent most of his ministry travelling with the twelve disciples, to whom he delegated much leadership responsibility: 'When Jesus had called the Twelve together, he gave them power and authority to drive out all demons and to cure diseases' (Lk. 9:1).

Then Jesus identifies a larger group of followers and sends them out in the same way as the Twelve: 'After this the Lord appointed seventy-two others and sent them two by two ahead of him to every town and place where he was about to go' (Lk. 10:1).

Not long after the time of Jesus' ascension we read: 'In those days Peter stood up among the believers (a group numbering about a hundred and twenty)' (Acts 1:15).

But the gospels refer to a 'crowd' or 'crowds' on over one hundred occasions. When Jesus was speaking people were flocking to see him, or following him, or being astounded by his miracles. Then there were the instances when Jesus fed five thousand and then four thousand men (plus women and children). There is no doubt that Jesus knew the importance of working with small numbers of people and large numbers of people.

He knew what it was like to have numbers of people desert him as well. Things seem to be going well in the first few verses of John 6: 'And a great crowd of people followed him because they saw the miraculous signs he had performed on the sick' (verse 2).

But by the end of the chapter, we read

> …'Yet there are some of you who do not believe.'
> For Jesus had known from the beginning which of them did not believe and who would betray him.
>   He went on to say, 'This is why I told you that no-one can come to me unless the Father has enabled him.'
>   From this time many of his disciples turned back and no longer followed him.
>   'You do not want to leave too, do you?' Jesus asked the Twelve (verses 64-67).

I strongly believe that the most important words of Jesus relating to the issue of numbers are the ones he uses when he sends out the seventy-two. In Luke 10:2 he tells them, 'The harvest is plentiful, but the workers are few. Ask the Lord of the harvest, therefore, to send out workers into his harvest field.'

With very few exceptions, the harvest field around every youth group is plentiful (the village group Gary mentioned at the start of the chapter might be one exception). I remember Ron Luce, from Teen Mania Ministries in the States, always emphasizing to youth leaders when he would speak to them that 'Jesus didn't just die for twelve quality people.' Jesus died for every person, and in our context every young person, in your town or city. Gary's right when he says the devil has the largest youth group, but Jesus demonstrated the love and the sacrifice that shows where God really wants all young people to belong, and that's in his family.

A youth leader says:
'Every size is important.'

Dream BIG and don't think small

I have heard it said that the first ingredient of success – the earliest spark in the dreaming youth – is this: dream a great dream.

John Alan Appleman, www.goal-setting-guide.com/quote-dream.html

Did you realize that God wants you to dream big dreams? Keeping the same size in a large successful youth group is actually thinking small and not dreaming big. I remember at the very same conference in Canada that I went to with Russ and Lara, hearing Judah Smith from Generation Church in Seattle speaking. Judah was speaking about the early days of his youth programme and said that from day one they dreamed big. To start with only a few young people came along, but the leaders had the mentality of developing something big for God, and before too long the group grew. Judah would imagine himself preaching to a crowded room of a thousand students when in fact only a small number were there in the first few weeks. Now his Wednesday night meeting has that crowded room.

A youth leader says:
'God wants us to be faithful with the small groups first before he'll trust us with the large numbers.'

There are big dreams all over the Bible: from Jacob's vision of a ladder, and Joseph seeing himself and his brothers binding sheaves of grain in Genesis, through to an angel appearing to Joseph the father of Jesus at numerous times in the nativity story told in the gospels. God can still speak through dreams and visions today, and without a God-given vision then things go badly wrong: 'When people do not accept divine guidance, they run wild. But whoever obeys the law is happy' (Prov. 29:18, NLT).

We'll talk more about vision in relation to leadership in Myth Four, but for now we are going to focus on having a big vision and dreaming a big dream. Here are two scriptural warnings. First Solomon reminds us of the main priority of dreaming godly dreams: 'So give your servant a discerning heart to govern your people and to distinguish between right and wrong. For who is able to govern this great people of yours?' (1 Kgs. 3:9).

Other translations prefer the phrase 'an understanding mind' instead of 'a discerning heart', but the advice is clear that what we are most seeking when we want to dream big dreams for youth ministry is wisdom. Secondly, in Ecclesiastes we are challenged to make sure we bring our dreams to fruition not simply by words but by hard work: 'Dreaming all the time instead of working is foolishness. And there is ruin in a flood of empty words' (Ecc. 5:7, NLT).

Let's finish our dreaming by looking at Peter's vision in Acts 10 – a vision that changed Peter's view, and the early church's view of Christianity from something restricted to 'Jews only' to something that was for Gentiles as well – in other words for everyone.

About noon the following day as they were on their journey and approaching the city, Peter went up on the roof to pray. He became hungry and wanted something to eat, and while the meal was being prepared, he fell into a trance. He saw heaven opened and something like a large sheet being let down to earth by its four corners. It contained all kinds of four-footed animals, as well as reptiles of the earth and birds of the air. Then a voice told him, 'Get up, Peter. Kill and eat.'

'Surely not, Lord!' Peter replied. 'I have never eaten anything impure or unclean.'

The voice spoke to him a second time, 'Do not call anything impure that God has made clean.'

This happened three times, and immediately the sheet was taken back to heaven (Acts 10:9-16).

This is some vision. Peter was given wisdom by God to discern what it meant and was brave enough to let God alter his complete outlook on life. It was a vision that radically enlarged Peter's faith. A few verses later we read, 'Then Peter began to speak:"I now realize how true it is that God does not show favouritism but accepts men from every nation who fear him and do what is right"' (verses 34,35).

The immediate consequence of Peter's vision was that the Holy Spirit was poured out on Gentile believers who were listening; the medium-term consequence was that Peter convinced the early church at the Council of Jerusalem in Acts 11 that Jesus had died so that everyone could believe and be saved. The longer-term consequences were that Peter reached out to the Jews, Paul to the Gentiles.

A youth leader says:
'Does my faith look big in this?'

✔ REALITY CHECK

1. What steps are you taking to make sure small groups are important?
2. What steps are you taking to increase the numbers in your youth group?
3. What are your BIG dreams for your ministry with young people?
4. How can God bring your dreams to reality?

MYTH 3

WE DON'T PREACH – WE ARE JUST SOWING THE SEEDS

Gary's Rant

Of all the myths we are attempting to debunk this is the one that I feel most passionate about. I was once the guest on a weekend away with a church youth group. We bundled the young people into a minibus and headed for a climbing wall. On the journey the leader, who was driving, regaled me with his philosophy of youth ministry. It's a number of years ago but the conversation is as fresh with me now as it was then.

'I don't preach to the kids,' he said, 'I don't force my views on them, but if any of them were to ask me why I was driving this minibus, I would tell them it was because I was a Christian.'

I remember being slack-jawed as I listened with amazement at the sheer stupidity of the statement. The immediate thought that ran through my mind was, 'What if they don't ask? Who's going to tell them about Jesus if you don't?' To this day I regret it remained a thought and not something I confronted this guy with. Thank goodness that countless

Christians throughout the ages did not have the same view. Chances are that the driver himself wouldn't have been sitting there at all were it not for someone who had spoken up to him.

There is also the thought often stated that as Christians there is something different about us. We have a 'different countenance' so they say. It's a suggestion that we have some sort of just-washed, rosy angelic glow. As if the sight of it is enough to convert the heathen or at worst prove to the world how holy we are. Don't get me wrong, I have met people like this but not everyone in my church looks like they should be members of the angelic host!

Seriously though, I suspect that to the kids I worked with I simply looked like a normal bloke. This just made me aware that if I did not share my faith through words, and not only through actions, they might miss the essence of the gospel. I might like to think my actions were always akin to Mother Teresa but what if sometimes the young people could justifiably call me a hypocrite or misunderstand my motives for a particular course of action? At times like this I can rely on the word of God to speak for itself.

The challenge must be not if to preach but when to preach. There always comes a point in the relationship you have developed with young people when you have sufficient credibility to earn a right to be heard. To be honest I actually think that for the many (and in my experience there are many) who cling to this myth like a Bible memory verse, they are actually using it as an excuse not to share their faith. It displays a lack of passion that I find frightening in those who claim to be called to work with young people.

Arguably, for some of us it does not come naturally to share our love for Jesus and his love for us by using words, and our fear of speaking to an assembled group of people might be very real. To this I would say learn how to do it. Learn how to verbally share your faith in a way that you feel comfortable with and just do it!

It may be convenient to blame the apparent inefficacy of preaching on attention spans shortened to a micro-second by our sound-bitten MTV culture, or on the shift to more interactive educational methods, but this focus on form entirely ignores the question of the relevance of the content. Surely, people who are expecting God to speak living words through his servant the preacher can remain attentive for twenty minutes? Surely, they will listen if they expect something vital to be said, something which might show them how to lead a life pleasing to God, how to fulfil their purpose on earth, to pursue the great adventure of faith?

Mark Greene, 'Can we preach today?' *LICC Magazine***, December 2003**

Preach the word

I'm convinced that one of the most important weapons in the armoury of anyone involved in youth ministry should be an ability to verbally communicate the Word of God. We must be willing to share our story with those around us. Real life stories, docu-soaps and fly-on-the-wall documentaries have never been more popular, and young people in particular can be captivated by a story. The Bible consistently reminds us that hand in hand with being a witness there is the opportunity to share our 'testimony' – our truthful telling of what God has done in our life.

Every believer should be able to do that, especially those involved in youth ministry. Yet more than that, I believe that powerful, passionate, Christ-centred, relevant preaching should be a priority for all who are called to youth ministry. Now you may contend that in a youth ministry 'team' not everyone needs to be a preacher – the gift of preaching can be represented by one or more individuals. I'll admit to a personal bias here because I spend a fair amount of my working life either speaking to young people, or training and equipping young people to speak to young people. In fact, when Gary and I were accepted into the work and ministry of Big Ideas in October 1995 verses from Paul's second letter to Timothy were read out at the commissioning service and they included these words: 'Preach the Word; be prepared in season and out of season; correct, rebuke and encourage – with great patience and careful instruction' (2 Tim. 4:2).

I've taken those verses to heart, and they have been the bedrock for all that I do. I've preached in churches packed with people, I've preached in churches full of empty spaces, I've preached to a handful of teenagers in a school CU, and I've preached to thousands of young people at concerts. I've preached when I've been 'up for it' and when I've felt it was the last thing I wanted to do. I've actively sought out opportunities to preach the good news of Jesus to young people – sometimes I've been given five minutes at a school assembly, other times I've been given six hours over a youth weekend; sometimes I've had an elaborate power point presentation ready, other times I've simply had my Bible. Sometimes, even though I say so myself, I've preached pretty well, and other times... well I'll leave that to your imagination. Most of all I've believed that preaching can make a difference in the lives of young people.

Let me tell you about Pete. When the Sound Nation Schools Mission came to Cardiff in 1998 Pete was sixteen. He came to every one of the follow-up meetings although he wasn't a Christian. We ran a café for ten weeks on a Thursday night, and Pete was at all of them. He would socialize with friends, enjoy the live music, and then dash out to the chip shop whenever things took a more serious turn. After a few weeks of this behaviour I'd spotted him, and eventually told him to sit down, shut up and listen to the speakers. For the first time in his life he actually listened to what people (myself included) were saying about Jesus.

Not long after the follow-up meetings finished, Pete gave his life to Christ and got baptized soon after that. Pete readily admits that what kept him at the cafés were definitely the friendship of caring Christians and the good quality of the live entertainment. He also believes that what God used to change his life was the preaching from a variety of leaders – he tells of how on more than one instance it was as if the speaker was speaking specifically to him. Pete is now in his early twenties; he worked as an intern with Ignite for eighteen months and now helps lead the youth group at his church, having recently completed the Ignite Leadership Academy. If I hadn't believed that those of us who were preaching at the Sound Nation café had something that was going to radically transform Pete then his life could have taken a very different course.

Most people become Christians under the age of eighteen. The 'Finding Faith' survey from 1994, although a bit dated now, claimed that seventy per cent of Christians gave their life to Christ under the age of twenty, with the peak being in the early teens. So it seems to me that it's vital to have dedicated people who can effectively communicate the good news to churched and unchurched young people alike. Now that's not a radical idea from me, that's a confirmation of Paul's priority.

How, then, can they call on the one they have not believed in? And how can they believe in the one of whom they have not heard? And how can they hear without someone preaching to them? And how can they preach unless they are sent? As it is written, 'How beautiful are the feet of those who bring good news!'

But not all the Israelites accepted the good news. For Isaiah says, 'Lord, who has believed our message?' Consequently, faith comes from hearing the message, and the message is heard through the word of Christ (Rom. 10:14-17).

A youth leader says:
'Preaching has become a bad word in youth ministry circles today. Perhaps we need to find a different word to replace it.'

Preaching might have a bad name today, but whatever terms we want to use we must realize that if we are serious about youth ministry we must be serious about 'preaching'. In Myth One we looked at the example of 'timespans' from the disciples in the book of Acts. Let's examine now the apostles' attitude to preaching.

In Acts 10 Peter is speaking to a large crowd in the house of Cornelius. Peter has dreamed his big dream about the message of Jesus being for everyone, and now he puts it into practice. At the end of his sermon the Holy Spirit comes upon both Jew and Gentile and new believers from both groups are baptized. In the middle of the sermon he says: 'He commanded us to preach to the people and to testify that he is the one whom God appointed as judge of the living and the dead' (verse 42).

The disciples were being obedient to a command of Jesus, just as we should be if we are truly his disciples. The commandment is to preach: some translations use the phrase 'announce clearly' or 'announce publicly', but the inference is still there that preaching is vital. In Acts 14 we learn that Paul and Barnabas have just spent time in Iconium and have been 'bravely speaking the message.' They have to escape for fear of their lives and so they go on to Lystra and Derbe 'where they continued to preach the good news' (verse 7).

Wherever Paul and the other apostles went, their focus remained the same – to share the gospel, or good news of Jesus. First this reminds us that preaching isn't just an occasional add-on to an already busy youth programme, but it is central to all that we do. Secondly, it reminds us above all that we preach good news. It is so easy to forget that, and to make our preaching sound as if it is bad news. Perhaps that's why preaching has become a dirty word in youth ministry: so often we don't do it justice.

In Acts 16, Paul and Silas are joined by Timothy. The writer Luke is travelling with them too: 'After Paul had seen the vision, we got ready at once to leave for Macedonia, concluding that God had called us to preach the gospel to them' (verse 10).

This verse makes it clear that preaching the gospel is a divine imperative. If we are called to youth ministry then we are under holy orders to tell the good news of Jesus to young people. It should be our priority, however contemporary and creative we want to be with it, to preach; and we need never apologize for taking the opportunity to impart even a few living words into young lives. Paul himself highlights this in his farewell talk to the leaders of the Ephesian church: 'You know that I have not hesitated to preach anything that would be helpful to you but have taught you publicly and from house to house' (Acts 20:20).

I once heard Bill Hybels, the senior pastor at Willow Creek Community Church, sharing his wisdom about preaching to seekers and to young people. He stated that normal expository preaching in church started in the world of the Bible passage and linked it to the world of everyday life. He then said that when speaking to seekers and young people it was wise to start off in the world of everyday life and then apply biblical truth to that. If Willow Creek has taught us something else then it is that modern media such as video, power point, drama and music can all enhance the message of the preacher, but they never replace the message.

Don't just talk the talk but walk the walk

Gary's frustration with this myth is that so many youth leaders think that they can walk young people into the kingdom of God just by example. We are saying that preaching is vital, but to redress the balance slightly it is important to recognize that nothing backs up powerful preaching like an exemplary lifestyle. We should all avoid the hypocrisy of the religious leaders at the time of Jesus. In Matthew 23 Jesus warned the crowds and his disciples: '…do not do what they do, for they do not practise what they preach' (verse 3).

> *It is no use walking anywhere to preach unless our walking is our preaching.*
>
> **St Francis of Assisi**

I want to melt this myth even more than just stating the case for preaching. The second half of the myth – 'we just sow the seeds' also allows for the carefree attitude of preaching the good news without allowing young people the opportunity to respond and to be nurtured.

Don't just sow but reap as well

The myth of just sowing the seeds perhaps comes from a superficial understanding of these verses in 1 Corinthians

> *I planted the seed, Apollos watered it, but God made it grow. So neither he who plants nor he who waters is anything, but only God, who makes things grow. The man who plants and the man who waters have one purpose, and each will be*

rewarded according to his own labour. For we are God's
fellow workers; you are God's field, God's building.
   By the grace God has given me, I laid a foundation as an
expert builder, and someone else is building on it. But each
one should be careful how he builds (1 Cor. 3:6-10).

Paul reminds us in this passage that any spiritual growth
in the life of a person is ultimately down to God, but he
also shows that God uses people of different gifts in the
growth process. To simply use these verses as authority
to 'sow the seed' and no more is to do a serious injustice to
the rest of Scripture. Paul's context for planting the seed
was very much preaching or proclamation. The parable
of the sower reminds us to be generous in the way we sow
the good news and we've already looked at these words of
Jesus in Myth 2: 'The harvest is plentiful, but the workers
are few. Ask the Lord of the harvest, therefore, to send out
workers into his harvest field' (Lk. 10:2).

Jesus is letting his followers know that they are not just
in the business of sowing seeds but in the business of
harvesting a crop too. The Bible is crammed full of
examples where God's spokesmen challenge listeners to
respond to what they have heard. Too often we have left
the harvesting to the well-known preachers at
conferences, concerts and large-scale youth events. We
have seen the J. John's and the Mike Pilavachi's encourage
our young people to respond to their preaching and we
have forgotten that a response could and should be part
and parcel of our own preaching. Here are a few biblical
calls to respond for you to consider. I'm not going to
unpack each one in great detail but you can open your
Bible and read them for yourself.

Exodus 32:19-26	Moses calls the disobedient Israelites
Joshua 24:15-27	Joshua issues a public call to commitment

1 Kings 18:21   Elijah makes a public invitation
2 Kings 23:3   King Josiah calls the people
Luke 19:5,6   Jesus calls Zacchaeus down from the tree

I'm really talking about what we variously term 'an altar call', 'a response', 'an appeal' or 'a time of ministry'. Actually I'm not too worried what we call it, but I am concerned that if we simply preach and give young people no opportunity to respond then we are not playing our full part as God's co-workers in the harvest. There are possibly many adults walking the streets of our country today who have heard the good news of Jesus but were never challenged to respond and so they didn't.

Let's turn again to the day of Pentecost where Peter 'makes his appeal': 'With many other words he warned them; and he pleaded with them, "Save yourselves from this corrupt generation." Those who accepted his message were baptised, and about three thousand were added to their number that day' (Acts 2:40,41).

Read these words and take them in: appeal, plead, exhort, urge, beg. These are the characteristics of the preacher when they seek to challenge listeners to respond to the voice of God. In various forms the word 'exhort' or its similar translation is found over a hundred times in the New Testament alone. For example in 2 Corinthians 5, Paul and Timothy 'try to persuade men'; they 'implore you on Christ's behalf' (verses 11,20).

That extreme should be a regular feature of our preaching too, and I'm not talking just about an evangelistic message that calls for a first-time commitment. When we are preaching to young believers and addressing issues of discipleship we should be demanding a response too. And you know what? Young people are used to making a response – how else do you think programmes like *Pop Idol* and *Fame Academy* are so successful? They know that teenagers who feel passionately enough about something will have the courage of their convictions – in this case voting for their preferred choice by text, phone or e-mail. Remember that one of the most important ingredients in any preaching, but especially to young people, is the mechanics by which they can respond to what God has been saying to them.

When Robert Moffat, a Scottish missionary in South Africa, came home to recruit helpers from the UK, he was greeted by a freezing British winter. Arriving at the church where he was due to preach, he was disappointed to see that only a small number of people had braved the elements to hear his appeal. What saddened him even more was there were only ladies that night, for he had chosen as his text, 'Unto you, O men, I call' (Prov. 8:4). When Moffat gave his appeal nobody answered the call or volunteered for missionary service. But what Moffat almost didn't see was a small boy in the loft who had come to work the bellows of the organ and was moved to respond to the message. The young boy decided he would become a missionary, went to school, studied medicine, and then went to Africa to reach people with the good news of Jesus. His name was David Livingstone.

I'll leave the last word to Mark Greene, from the LICC, because he melts this myth succinctly and in a way that acts as a useful summary of all we have been discussing in this chapter

I'm enthusiastic about the future of preaching, convinced that the Bible can speak today and tomorrow. I am convinced that we can preach today if we delve deep into Scripture. We can preach today if we really know our people. We can preach today using established forms and hopefully new forms too. We can preach today if we preach whole-life Christianity, if we don't lose our confidence in the authority God has given us to warn and encourage every person so that they may grow up in maturity, into the fullness of Christ. We can preach today if we don't pretend that preaching can do it all. We can preach today if we ensure that there are other effective teaching ministries in place to address the legitimate discipleship needs of individuals. We can preach today if we recognize that it is not our rhetoric, our powerpoint, or our scholarship that will liberate and transform people's hearts. We can preach today if we trust in the power of God's word and the Spirit to do the work. Thank God, he still does.

Mark Greene, 'Can we preach today?' *LICC Magazine* **December.2003**

✔ REALITY CHECK

1. How often are the young people in your group exposed to preaching aimed specifically for them?
2. What steps should you take to improve your preaching/public speaking gifts?
3. Are there other leaders in your team whose preaching/public speaking gifts you should be developing?
4. What ways could you more consistently build 'responses' into your preaching and teaching?

MYTH 4

YOU HAVE TO ASK THEM WHAT THEY WANT

When I was in the first few years of youth ministry, 'participation' was a popular word. It meant that you had to involve young people in decision making, in programme planning and in dictating the agenda. Every September I would sit down with a bunch of teenagers and attempt the 'participation' process. Results varied from a blank piece of paper to a list of suggestions unprintable in a Christian book. I gradually realized that I'd been abdicating responsibility and that vision, direction and planning needed to come from me as a leader, and then participation and involvement from the young people themselves became a real possibility. The myth of 'you have to ask them what they want' is really about those words: leadership, responsibility, vision and then participation.

A youth leader says:
'They want sex but we're not going to give it to them!'

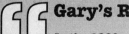 **Gary's Rant**

In the 1960s, youth work, which had long been the preserve of the voluntary sector, was suddenly on the government agenda. State funding was made available which led to the setting up of colleges for youth workers in order that the people interested in working with young people could receive qualifications. What had been at best a calling and at worst a hobby could now be professionalized. In many ways this was a good thing for youth work. However, when the new 'professionals' looked at organizations such as the Scouts and Guides and other voluntary sector youth groups, they wrongly concluded that much of the work revolved around telling young people what to do. So a different paradigm began to develop: it suggested that workers should ask young people what they wanted to do and act on this. This summary of recent history is intentionally simplistic but we have lost sight of a significant factor about Christian youth ministry that I believe needs to be redressed. A key ingredient of youth ministry must be that our relationship with God will inform us of what young people want.

I want you to understand something: in Ignite we are not fundamentally against what trendy youth workers call 'participation', but we are committed to guiding and involving young people in decisions that they are able to take. Let me tell you a story.

In the late 1980s, animal activists decided that it was cruel to keep hens in battery cages and that the solution was to release the fowl and allow them to escape. So one dark night, they targeted a particularly large farm with tens of thousands of birds. They opened the sheds, unfastened the cages and took the hens and released them into the farmyard. Next morning all the hens were dead. They hadn't been killed by foxes but had frozen to death. You see battery hens are not used to having so many choices. Everything they needed to survive previously had been provided for them: food, light and heat. In the farmyard they did not make a bolt for freedom in some daring Chicken Run style escape; they just stood still, wondered why there was no food, assumed as it was dark they should go to sleep, and froze to death.

What does this have to do with youth ministry? Simply that often we are so used to telling young people what they will do and when they will do it that when we ask what they want, they simply do not understand the question. The best you can hope for is a superficial answer. No sane parent asks a toddler what he or she wants in a sweet shop. The choice is too vast, they do not understand the value of money and they are not equipped to respond articulately. Rather, the sensible parent asks something like 'crisps or chocolate?'

Back to the animal activists! They now know if they want to release battery hens it is a much more difficult process. They have to take the birds to a safe environment and put them in a slightly bigger battery cage. When they are used to this they increase its size and continually do this until they can release them into a barn. Only when they are safe to do this do they allow them to forage as free-range birds.

My point is simply this: leaders should be on their face before God asking for revelation of a vision about what he requires for the work. Once they receive this vision it should be then incarnated in the work, allowing young people to shape not the vision but the process of how the vision is achieved. No animal activist ever asked a chicken if it wanted to be released, they worked through their passionate belief to do the right thing. I think we can learn something from this. You are called to work with young people: they are not called to work with you!

You've got to lead

To melt this myth effectively you will have to recognize that if you have been called to leadership you must lead. You must seek God for a vision, build that vision, make it a reality and lead young people. One of the most obvious definitions of a leader is someone who people follow. There are many different styles of leadership but the result should be the same – young people will follow you. When Paul is writing to the church in Rome he reminds them of the importance of effective leadership

God has given each of us the ability to do certain things well. So if God has given you the ability to prophesy, speak out when you have faith that God is speaking through you. If your gift is that of serving others, serve them well. If you are a teacher, do a good job of teaching. If your gift is to encourage others, do it! If you have money, share it generously. If God has given you leadership ability, take the responsibility seriously. And if you have a gift for showing kindness to others, do it gladly. (Rom. 12:6-8, emphasis added, NLT)

A youth leader says:
'Over-reliance on young people themselves to provide programme and identity for the group only goes to show a lack of real leadership.'

You are a minister – you are a leader

Sometimes Paul was criticized for taking himself too seriously and for constantly reminding people that he operated under the authority of Jesus. It seems to me that Paul was just taking his calling seriously and recognizing that God had placed into his hands a job that required much responsibility and determination. Paul also realized that any real progress was always going to involve the Holy Spirit.

If you are committed to youth ministry then you are a specialist and you are operating under God's calling. You are a minister. Whether you are full-time, part-time, a volunteer with an armful of qualifications or no qualifications; you are a minister of the gospel. Time and time again Paul tells us that we are 'God's fellow-workers'.[i] In Peter's first letter we read words that indicate how importantly we should take our role as fellow workers with God: 'But you are the ones chosen by God, chosen for the high calling of priestly work, chosen to be a holy people, God's instruments to do his work and speak out for him' (1 Pet. 2:9, *The Message*).

Whatever your church thinks about youth ministry, whatever others think of your role, however downtrodden you might feel at times, however poorly treated you might be, remember that you have been called by God to serve as a co-worker with Jesus, and you are serving in the mission field of young people.

Amongst the multitude of advice and support Paul offers Timothy we find these two verses

If you point these things out to the brothers, you will be a good minister of Christ Jesus, brought up in the truths of the faith and of the good teaching that you have followed' (1 Tim. 4:6).

But you should keep a clear mind in every situation. Don't be afraid of suffering for the Lord. Work at bringing others to Christ. Complete the ministry God has given you' (2 Tim. 4:5, NLT).

In Paul's view, the younger Timothy should concentrate on being a 'good minister' and completing the ministry God has given him. In order to 'complete' we will need to be people with vision, with leadership and with a passion to fulfil the mission God has called us to.

A youth leader says:
'We should be asking Jesus what they need, not the young people themselves. What they want and what they need aren't the same thing.'

You are a minister – you are a servant

The phrase 'good minister' in 1 Timothy 4:6 means a servant attitude, and the phrase 'complete the ministry' often translated 'discharge all the duties of your ministry', means to pack everything that you do in the name of Jesus with all the passion, experience, commitment, enthusiasm, study, wisdom and compassion that you can muster. If we are co-workers with God then we should give it everything we have got. Youth ministry deserves no less than any other God-appointed ministry in the church. The option of giving less than one hundred per cent is just not on. The teenage girl with parents going through a divorce, the young man suffering physical abuse, the guy struggling with exams at school, the girl desperately trying to be a witness to her non-Christian friends: don't they all deserve excellence from you?

In fact, the apostle Paul tells us that we should be wholehearted, and strive for excellence in everything that we do, not just 'our ministry': 'And whatever you do, whether in word or deed, do it all in the name of the Lord Jesus, giving thanks to God the Father through him' (Col. 3:17).

'Whatever you do, work at it with all your heart, as working for the Lord, not for men' (Col. 3:23).

In the context of the letter, Paul is giving advice to those who may be in slavery and he's telling them that however tough their daily work is that they should do it as if it is actually for the Lord himself. Now if the Bible tells slaves to work hard, as if for the Lord, then consider what our attitude should be to serving in the church. Bible scholars look at the verse above and conclude that they mean Christians should do everything in dependence on the Lord, recognizing the authority of the name of Jesus, and serving faithfully in the name of Jesus.

In the second book of Chronicles we read of Solomon becoming king. As soon as it is apparent that Solomon will take over from his father David, we read of this encounter between Solomon and the Lord God

> *That night God appeared to Solomon and said to him, 'Ask for whatever you want me to give you.' Solomon answered God, 'You have shown great kindness to David my father and have made me king in his place. Now, LORD God, let your promise to my father David be confirmed, for you have made me king over a people who are as numerous as the dust of the earth.* Give me wisdom and knowledge, that I may lead this people, for who is able to govern this great people of yours?' *(2 Chr. 1:7-10, emphasis added).*

Solomon could have asked the Lord for anything and he chose to ask for the wisdom and knowledge to be a leader. He became one of the wisest men to ever live, and one of the greatest kings.

A youth leader says:
'This is my passion, this is my life! I want to lead these young people to the place God wants them to go.'

What is a leader? Here are some paraphrases of definitions I have found.

A leader is:
- A person who has the ability to get others to do what they don't want to do and like it (Anon).
- A person who is willing to take more than their fair share of the blame and less of their fair share of the credit (Anon).
- A person who has the courage to take action whilst others hesitate (John Maxwell).
- An ordinary person with extraordinary determination (Anon).
- A person who knows where he wants to go, and gets up, and goes (John Erskine).
- A person who is close enough to relate to others, but far enough ahead to motivate them (John Maxwell).
- A dealer in hope (Napoleon).

God put me on earth to accomplish a certain number of things. Right now I'm so far behind I will never die!

Anon

Get your vision

We talked in Myth Two about dreaming dreams and getting visions. A clear vision for your ministry is vital. In the King James translation we read: 'Where there is no vision, the people perish' (Prov. 29:18).

The NIV translations says that where there is no revelation the people cast off restraint, whilst the NLT states that when people do not accept divine guidance they run wild. Time alone with God, or with your leadership team seeking God collectively, in order to get a vision, refine a vision, or seek a new vision, is never time wasted.

Leadership is the capacity to translate vision into reality.

Warren G. Bennis, www.quoteproject.com

In simplest terms, a leader is one who knows where he wants to go, and gets up, and goes.

John Erskine, The Complete Life

Make your mission statement

The story is told of General George Patton, the famous American soldier in World War II. When inspecting his troops he would regularly approach individual soldiers and ask, 'What is your mission, soldier?' The soldier was in very hot water if he couldn't come up with an answer, because Patton expected everyone to know what they were doing and why they were doing it. My friend Ron Luce, founder of Teen Mania Ministries, asks a similar question of youth pastors at his Acquire the Fire conferences. He asks, 'What is your priority?' and then answers his own question by saying 'David's and Mary's, those are your priorities.' He means that youth pastors should be determined to produce young men with the same heart as David; young men who will stand up to the giants of this world in the name of the Lord: 'David said to the Philistine, "You come against me with sword and spear and javelin, but I come against you in the name of the LORD Almighty, the God of the armies of Israel, whom you have defied"' (1 Sam. 17:45).

And young women who will display the same obedience to the voice of God as Mary did: '"I am the Lord's servant," Mary answered. "May it be to me as you have said." Then the angel left her' (Lk. 1:38).

In John 4 Jesus encounters the Samaritan woman at the well. At the end of this amazing story she heads off into the local town to tell everyone about this incredible person she has just met. The disciples also headed off into the same town, but they were more concerned about finding food to fill their bellies. So it's possible to head in the right direction but with the wrong priority. A 'mission statement' will help you with direction and priority that you have for the young people God has called you to lead.

If you haven't already got a mission statement for your youth ministry and for your own calling then I strongly advise you to construct one. It will be something that concisely and powerfully explains what you are about and will help you focus on the priority to which you believe God has called you.

The ministry IGNITE that Gary and I direct has this mission statement:

Ignite challenges young people to discover God's purpose in their life, to be a disciple of Jesus and to transform their generation.

Breaking it down we see that it:
- Starts with the name of the ministry.
- Reminds us we are about 'challenging' current forms of thinking and attitude.
- Focuses us on 'young people' as our target group.
- Identifies the three key areas we want to challenge young people with: God's purpose for their life, living as a disciple of Jesus and transforming their generation. In other words equipping and releasing young people to witness into their own peer groups.

A few years ago I reached a crisis point in my own walk with God as far as ministry and calling went. I'd been in youth ministry for years, then concentrated on evangelism and then more recently had been involved in discipleship. What exactly was I? A youth pastor, an evangelist or a discipler? I can remember lying in bed in a hotel room in the early hours of the morning with the singer Paul Colman lying in the next bed. We had just finished working on tour with the band Third Day and were due to fly our separate ways in the morning.

He asked me a simple question, 'How would you describe what you do?' I stumbled around trying to find the appropriate words before Paul offered me his own answer: 'I'll tell you what you do,' he said, 'you encourage people to follow Jesus.' I swiftly gave my thanks to Paul and to God, because in that sentence he'd clarified for me what I had been trying to come to terms with myself. Ever since then my personal mission statement has been *'Encouraging people to follow Jesus.'*

I break it down like this:
- *Encouraging* – ministry must be positive and attractive, helping others.
- *People* – above all it's people focused, not plans or programmes.
- *To follow* – either to start or to continue a lifelong journey of Christian discipleship.
- *Jesus* – he's the reason I do what I do and I am who I am.

Sometimes your mission statement might need to be more specific. In January 2003, Matt Gregor, a twenty-three year old, started working with me two days a week. I've known Matt since he was sixteen and he's been a key volunteer on our Ignite summer mission teams for the last five years. The church that Matt and I are members of entered into an agreement with Ignite that Matt would be youth pastor at the church, but would be mentored by myself. Over the first couple of weeks we talked and prayed about Matt's role as youth pastor. He was desperate to establish a new vision for the youth ministry and to create a mission statement for it. Instead we initially focused just on his priorities and this is what we came up with

What type of person do I want to be in order to do what God's got planned for me?

Personal priorities:
- Strengthening my personal relationship with Jesus.
- Seeing the under-eighteens grow in Christ and serve him.
- Shaping youth ministry in church into a strong identity.
- Supporting the team of volunteer leaders in the church and give direction.
- Spreading the vision for youth ministry in the church.
- Sharpening my skills in youth ministry and putting them into practice.

If you have a strong, God-given vision, earthed in a manageable mission statement you'll find that your leadership team and young people will soon catch on and believe in you, your vision, and the God that gave it to you in the first place.

A youth leader says:
'I believe in giving young people choices, but I believe we should be giving them guided choices and showing them the best direction to travel.'

Leadership and learning are indispensable to each other.
John F. Kennedy in a speech prepared for delivery in Dallas on the day of his assassination, 22 November 1963

Help young people grow as leaders

All the above emphasis on the importance of youth leaders taking seriously their role, might give you the impression that we believe that young people are simply to be led like sheep. Well nothing could be further from the truth. I hope you will have seen from the example of Matt above that we really recognize the vital importance of developing, training, equipping and releasing younger leaders. Someone once defined Christian leadership as any influence that any individual has on any other individuals or any group for the glory of God – so young people definitely have a part to play.

I'm writing this chapter in the Christmas holidays of 2003 and over the last week or so I've been receiving e-mails from teenagers who live all over Wales. They have been letting me know that they are coming to a weekend we have planned for emerging leaders linked into the Flames of Fire conference that we are involved in each summer. At the end of January we are gathering twenty or so older teenagers to begin to work with them as leaders of the youth programme at Flames of Fire over the coming years.

As I write, we are just a few weeks away from commencing with the second intake of our Ignite Leadership Academy. Twice a year, for one night a week over twelve weeks, and for a residential weekend, we train a dozen or so sixteen to twenty-two year olds in Christian leadership. This is the mission statement for the Academy: 'The Ignite Leadership Academy trains young people to impact their generation by challenging them to become inspirational leaders.'

One session of the Leadership Academy is given over completely to vision, mission statement, setting goals and targets. For Gary and myself, and for Peter and Sandra Brind who head up the academy, we want to lead our academy students with all the ability God has given us and we want to see a generation of Mary's and David's who will impact those around them by becoming, and living as inspirational leaders. Remember the old cliché about the difference between a boss and a leader? A boss says 'Go!' but a leader says 'Let's go!'

✔REALITY CHECK

1. How can you become a more effective leader?
2. If you have a mission statement, re-read it and amend if necessary. If you don't have one then ask the Lord to give you wisdom to develop one.
3. What ways could you encourage participation from your young people?
4. Begin to identify the next generation of youth leaders.

Notes

 i See for example 1 Cor. 3:9, 2 Cor. 6:1 and 1 Thes. 3:2.

MYTH 5

YOUNG PEOPLE LACK COMMITMENT

Gary's Rant

I was born in the 1960s. When it came to leisure time activities there were very few options. It was totally about which groups my friends attended, and almost all of the limited options were based around the local church. They were the only show in town. Rejecting these options would commit you to a life sitting in a bedroom that consisted of a bed and a wardrobe (and a brother!), watching one of the three channels on the black and white TV or hanging around the street corner.

Society is different in the twenty-first century. I am now a parent. My children are involved in a variety of sports clubs, church-based youth activities and tuition in a variety of musical instruments. Their choice is vast. One of my jobs as a parent is to limit the options for my kids not expand them. Sometimes I have to persuade my eldest child to leave her bedroom, complete with TV and video; remove her from the internet or dissuade her from texting her friends when she could meet them if she were prepared to step out of the front door.

The days of church being the only show in town are long gone. Leisure providers recognize the power of the young wallet. It matters not to them whether the cash comes directly from the young person or via their parents' pockets. The range is vast and can include sports clubs, health and leisure clubs, multiplex cinemas and many more.

The central question is: do young people lack commitment? I would argue that they lack commitment to things that are less than excellent, because they have a choice. Their parents, in a desire to keep their offspring happy and fulfilled, are more likely to encourage them to move on if they display any dissatisfaction with their present activities.

As a young man I agreed to take a group of young people away with a larger group on a camping trip. The agreement was that the young people could go if I was there. A month before we were due to go I was told by my boss he would not give me the time off. This put the whole trip in jeopardy. I reached a compromise with the camp leader. If he would allow my group to attend I would travel to the camp each night and commute back to work each day. When the young people found out my intentions the relationship between us went up several gears. From this point these lads would do anything I asked of them. In their mind I had shown total commitment to them, giving them a holiday that they had never had before.

The challenge to those called to youth ministry is not to settle for second best when it comes to delivering a quality programme. However, the thing that could give us the edge is when we show a commitment to young people: they may not see this from any other direction and agency.

A youth leader says:
'Is it us who lack commitment to young people?'

If our experience of Christian youth ministry has always been a steady pattern of decline then we might easily fall for the myth that young people lack commitment. Globally, however the story is very different. If we were to tell advertisers and marketing executives that young people lack commitment they would laugh in our faces, for they know that if you can capture the imagination of a person when they are young then the likelihood is you will have their brand loyalty for life.

Experts in postmodernism confirm that as far as the current generation goes, commitment to organizations and denominations is very much a thing of the past, but loyalty and commitment to a cause or to a group of like-minded people is a hallmark of today's teens and young adults. At the Children's Earth Summit in Johannesburg in 2002, a seventeen-year-old called Jessica Rimington decided to organize a movement called the Young People's Decade of Commitment. This is what she said

The summit helped me realize that young people really can make a difference, and that if we speak up, people will listen. We don't have to wait until we are adults to accomplish something, to help, to find a passion and to work toward our dreams. Just as our action can have a positive effect on the world, our inaction can have a negative effect. No matter what we are doing, we are making a difference. It is up to each of us to decide what kind of difference we choose to make. Those involved in the Young People's Decade of Commitment have made their choice and are affecting positive change everyday.

Extreme commitment – the Ignite Declaration

Fortunately, many of us recognize this type of extreme commitment in Christian teenagers as well. The heart of the Ignite initiative is the Ignite Declaration – a six-part discipleship commitment that we have been challenging young people to sign up to and to live their life on. At the time of writing we have over two thousand five hundred young people around Cardiff and in other parts of the UK who have signed the declaration.

Here is the declaration in its entirety

I believe that God has a special purpose for my generation and me. I ask God to ignite in me a desire to discover this purpose.

I commit to:

Include Jesus in my moral life, my thoughts, words, actions and relationships.

Grow closer to Jesus through studying the Bible, praying and allowing the Holy Spirit to lead me each day.

Network with other Christians in my city, my country and throughout the world.

Involve myself in a local church and respect its leadership.

Take the message of Jesus into my school, college or place of work and the world by praying, living and witnessing so that everyone may have an opportunity to know Jesus.

Explore God's will for myself and my generation and seek to follow it.

When young people catch hold of this vision for radical, extreme, ignited living for Jesus then they really show a deep level of commitment – one that you would expect from someone living as a disciple of Jesus. Throughout the year we regularly get letters or e-mails from young people telling us what God has been doing through them. Here's a recent e-mail that arrived in our office

> *I'd just like to give you some feedback about how God's been working in my life and a lot in my friends lives! At least ten of my friends have become Christians just through me chatting to them about Jesus and inviting them along to meetings and youth events. Over the last year Jesus has become the biggest part of my life, thoughts, words, actions and relationships and I've grown closer to him every day. I go to boarding school so living in such close relations to other girls it is very hard for people not to notice how you live your life. I've now reached the point where the two girls I share a room with ask me to pray with them every night, and we do our daily Bible readings together. Our CU has grown massively this term!*
>
> *I believe God is moving in a massive way among youth especially today. My testimony is just one of millions of other young Christians around this country. Those simple little Ignite cards give people like me something to focus on, and they are a small reminder of how to live our lives to glorify the Lord.*
>
> **Anneka, fourteen**

A youth leader says:
'Most of the young people in my group are more committed than their parents are.'

You can build commitment

It is clear that when young people are faced with the challenge of a cause to believe in and an opportunity to serve, then many respond positively. Your challenge is to build that commitment up and make it strong. If the challenge of a personal relationship with Jesus and the joy of following him are revealed as a no-holds-barred approach to life, then you'll see a level of commitment from teenagers of biblical proportions.

Of course, it is true to say that some young people will not be able to translate their enthusiasm and excitement into long-term commitment, but that is a trait of the human race and not just the younger generation. Perhaps the struggle for those of us in youth ministry is that young people often seem committed to different priorities whether they are Christians or not. The seventeen-year old guy who is up till the early hours of the morning playing an online computer game with a friend is showing a high level of commitment. The girl who attends school musical rehearsals four nights a week as well as doing her homework is showing dedication and commitment. Christians in your youth group may be committed to causes, or groups of people, or events, or bands, all of which enhance their life as a disciple, but none of which give them greater commitment to you or to your youth group.

Now I believe that young people should be committed to a local church and to the people in that local church, but more than that I believe they should be committed to Jesus and to a life of discipleship. This means that every so often you and your youth group and your church might 'suffer' because of the commitment to Christ that some of your young people show.

A good example of this would be a girl I know called Becky. She's from a small Baptist church in West Wales, where her father is the pastor. Becky is a girl of outstanding commitment to Jesus, and as I write she is on a YWAM discipleship training school – in fact she's completing the mission part of the school and is somewhere in Bosnia. Now Becky believes in the local church. She was a committed leader of the youth ministry in her church when she was at home, and without her the youth work has been more demanding for her parents. Yet everybody recognizes that despite leaving a gap in the church, Becky hasn't displayed a lack of commitment to the church, her youth group, or her parents: she's demonstrated complete faith and trust in God as she steps out to serve him. She is showing that one of the most powerful levels of commitment young Christians can show is a commitment to reach their own generation for Jesus.

We should be people who can teach, model, develop and build commitment. This means we learn to see young people as having plenty of potential for commitment rather than plenty of potential for broken promises.

> *Praise youth and it will prosper.*
>
> **Irish Proverb**

One thing I have tried to do consistently in ministry is to 'let my yes be yes and my no be no' (Mt. 5:37). I mean that when I commit to do something I do it, I follow it through, I fulfil that diary date, I make that phone call, I pray for the person who asked me to. It means sometimes I have to say 'no' when it would be easier to say 'yes' but not bother to follow through with it. That's one small way to model commitment.

Biblical models

Another important way of building commitment into the lives of young people is to teach biblical models. There are oodles of young people in the Bible who display outstanding levels of commitment in their walk with God, and they can be used as shining examples today. Here are just four.

Josiah

From the age of eight, Josiah was King of Judah. He reigned for thirty-one years. The king before him lasted two years, and the king after him lasted three months! So Josiah must have been doing something right. In 2 Kings 23 we read of the key incident in his life. He's twenty-six at the time, and one of his servants finds the book of the Law in the Temple and brings it to Josiah. Rather than ignore it, auction it, give it back to the Temple priests or stick it in a museum, Josiah reads it and as a consequence realizes the spiritual mess his country is in. After he had read the word of God, he took action. He tore down the idols that had been built in the Temple, rubbished the shops that had been built in the Temple grounds, threw out the priests from other religions and even killed some of them. In fact he did everything he could to get rid of anything that stood in the way of the Israelites worshipping God. This is what the Bible says about Josiah: 'Neither before nor after Josiah was there a king like him who turned to the LORD as he did – with all his heart and with all his soul and with all his strength, in accordance with all the Law of Moses' (2 Kgs. 23:25).

Now that's commitment. In Josiah's case, his commitment to the Lord was to cost him his life. Only a few verses after the one above, we read that Josiah was killed in a battle against the enemies of Israel.

Esther

Esther was a young girl who foiled a plot to exterminate the whole Jewish nation. Had the plot succeeded, the immediate consequences would have been no Nehemiah, and the longer-term consequences would have been no Jesus! I want to give a name check here to Naomi and Lois – two great biblical names but actually two young women

who have worked with me in Ignite and who have
passionately and faithfully told the story of Esther to many
other young girls. If it wasn't for Na and FloJo I wouldn't
be writing about Esther now.

Esther's story is set at the time of the Jewish exile and
when the Persian King Xerxes needs a new queen, he
chooses Esther from among a group of girls that have been
captured and brought to the palace for his pleasure. Esther
kept her Jewish nationality a secret, and when she was
queen heard of a scheme that the new Prime Minister, a
man called Haman, had convinced the king was a good one
– a plot to wipe out all Jews. Esther wasn't able to talk with
King Xerxes unless he summoned her, but she took the risk
and went to see him, she revealed her heritage and
potentially signed her own death warrant. Instead of killing
Esther, the king executed Haman on the very same gallows
that he'd erected to kill Mordecai who was Esther's uncle.
Throughout her story, Mordecai was an inspiration,
challenge and encouragement to Esther and the King had
wanted rid of him. Oh yes, I forgot to mention this as well as
giving up her virginity to the King when she was in his
harem, Esther was also the subject of a nasty assault from
Haman. In reply to her uncle's plea to help the Jewish
nation, Esther says this: '"Go, gather together all the Jews
who are in Susa, and fast for me. Do not eat or drink for
three days, night or day. I and my maids will fast as you do.
When this is done, I will go to the king, even though it is
against the law. And if I perish, I perish"' (Esth. 4:16).

Sacrifice, selflessness, compassion for her people, and a
readiness to make a difference were all hallmarks of
Esther's commitment. Her commitment, and trust in God,
made her a heroine.

Mary the mother of Jesus

Mary is an unmarried teenager when the angel Gabriel
pays her a visit. Despite his comforting words, Mary is

initially very frightened and then extremely perplexed when Gabriel reveals to her that she is to give birth to the Son of God. We have already heard about Mary's final response in Myth Four. She takes on board the enormity of Gabriel's message very quickly and pledges her loyalty and obedience to the Lord.

For the next few months Mary has to live with an incredible secret, has to deal with family, has to sort things out with Joseph, her fiancé and then has to endure a long journey on a donkey before giving birth to Jesus in a stable. As if that wasn't enough she then has to escape with husband and baby to Egypt, before her newborn son is killed by Herod.

Before their escape to Egypt, Mary and her family are visited by wise men and by shepherds. The shepherds can't wait to go off and tell everyone the good news. Mary has a different approach: 'But Mary treasured up all these things and pondered them in her heart' (Lk. 2:19)

Even as a young girl, Mary realized that her commitment was going to be long-term. She was ready to give the rest of her life to Jesus, and understood too, that the best way to prepare to serve God was by making a heart response. For Mary, her extreme experience of bringing the Messiah into the world was one that she was going to treasure for all time.

Timothy

We don't have loads of information about Timothy, but what we do have is quality. He started serving God when he was a young man; he was loved by some very spiritual people in his family, he spent loads of time with Paul on the frontlines of early Christianity and his name meant 'to honour God.' Just as Lois and Naomi love to talk about Esther, I love to talk about Paul and Timothy. In fact one of the first sermons that Matt Gregor and I shared together was about Paul and Timothy. It was great fun talking about a relationship that we ourselves were trying to model as well.

Timothy was invited by Paul to travel with him. What an incredible opportunity. Yet there was a problem. Timothy's father was Greek, and Timothy had not been circumcised. Paul was going to be meeting Jews all over the place, and travelling with a Gentile who hadn't been circumcised would be too big a risk to take. So Timothy showed his commitment by getting circumcised: 'so Paul wanted him to join them on their journey. In deference to the Jews of the area, he arranged for Timothy to be circumcised before they left, for everyone knew that his father was a Greek' (Acts 16:3, NLT).

This was a massive commitment on two counts. First, both Jews and Gentiles prided themselves on their viewpoint, so Timothy was risking his relationship with his father. Secondly, circumcision was normally performed on young babies and for a young man it was an extremely painful operation. This initial commitment led to Timothy becoming a close friend and partner in the gospel with Paul, to him living a different life than other young men, and it also led to him being thrown in prison. It eventually led to Paul handing the baton of ministry over to his younger colleague Timothy.

These are just four examples of committed young people in the Bible. I could have told you about David, Jonathan, Isaac, Joseph, Jeremiah, about Naaman's servant girl, John Mark and the boy with five loaves and two fish. You can find out all about them for yourself.

✔ REALITY CHECK

1. Are there ways that you and your youth leaders could demonstrate more commitment to your young people?
2. Are you demanding commitment from young people in the wrong priority areas?
3. How can you 'build commitment' more effectively?
4. Check out the Ignite discipleship declaration at www.igniteme.org

MYTH 6

YOUNG PEOPLE ARE THE FUTURE OF THE CHURCH

To get back to my youth I would do anything in the world, except take exercise, get up early, or be respectable.

Oscar Wilde, *The Picture of Dorian Gray*, 1891

❝❝ Gary's Rant

If you have been in youth ministry for any length of time I am sure that some well meaning old lady or man from your congregation has come up to you after a morning service and uttered the immortal lines, 'Young people are the future of this church.'

Now please understand, it is meant as an encouragement. They are saying it to build you up. They are supportive of your work and they have a genuine affection for the young people. Nevertheless, the only course of action open to you is to beat them senseless with a dog-eared copy of Mission Praise until they repent of the lie that emanates from the darkest pit of hell!

The problem with this statement is although it is well meaning it places the young people in deficit, suggesting that their qualification for being an effective disciple is to reach a specific age. This is not only unhelpful; it is also unbiblical. Many of those that Jesus originally called were only teenagers themselves. On these he built his church. What we know and must shout from the highest steeple, pulpit or overhead projector stand is that young people are part of the church today.

How do we help develop these young people to ensure their ministry comes into its fullness? A number of years ago, I attended a major Christian conference for the first time. It was very impressive. What encouraged me was that the main guy in leadership stood on the last night and from the stage, looked over his platform party and said, 'By next year many of these people will have gone and we are going to fill this platform with younger people.' I was so impressed. I thought this is what church should be about: older people standing aside and encouraging a rising generation into positions of responsibility.

For a few months I was the biggest advocate for this event, based primarily on this story. This all changed one day. I was preaching in a church and they had a tape library. There was a tape from the same conference. However, it was from ten years previously. I borrowed the tape and to my delight it was the same guy preaching (it was also the same guy leading worship). To be fair it was a great sermon but my heart sank at the end when the leader uttered the words: 'By next year many of these people will have gone and we are going to fill this platform with younger people.' At this point I realized that this was a piece of rhetoric that had been trotted out for years and, to my knowledge, never enacted.

> As older people we have to begin to take risks and one of the major ones is to step aside. It may be that the young person stepping into our shoes might be not be able to do the job as effectively as us. However this is no excuse for stopping their progress. Of course it could be that they are more effective at the job than us...

Which would be worse?

We cannot always build the future for our youth, but we can build our youth for the future.

Franklin D. Roosevelt

Purely potentials?

If the church keeps on believing this myth about young people, then there will be no young people left around in the future to be the church. This is a 'whole church' problem and not just a youth ministry one. In the last chapter we saw some young people in the Bible who displayed outstanding commitment. Other young people in the Bible, for one reason or another, weren't initially able to contribute as fully to God's people.

Their drawback was that in the eyes of some they were purely potential for the future, which would have meant that God's plan for them to be involved in the present could have been compromised.

Joshua – a long apprenticeship

Joshua faced the frustration of being earmarked for leadership and then having to wait a long, long time for that to come to fruition. God spoke to Moses and made it clear that Joshua would inherit the leadership of the Israelite people:

Because of you the LORD became angry with me also and said, 'You shall not enter it, either. But your assistant, Joshua son of Nun, will enter it. Encourage him, because he will lead Israel to inherit it. And the little ones that you said would be taken captive, your children who do not yet know good from bad – they will enter the land. I will give it to them and they will take possession of it (Deut. 1:37-39).

It became clear that Joshua had been earmarked for the future and had to serve out his time as Moses' potential successor for a big chunk of his adult life. Moses was eighty at the time, but was still leading the people forty years later: 'Then Moses went out and spoke these words to all Israel:"I am now a hundred and twenty years old and I am no longer able to lead you. The LORD has said to me, 'You shall not cross the Jordan'" (Deut. 31:1,2).

Not long after this, Moses handed over the leadership to Joshua and then died. The Lord spoke to Joshua and confirmed the job that he had for him

After the death of Moses the servant of the LORD, the LORD said to Joshua son of Nun, Moses' assistant: 'Moses my servant is dead. Now then, you and all these people, get ready to cross the Jordan River into the land I am about to give to them – to the Israelites. I will give you every place where you set your foot, as I promised Moses (Josh. 1:1-3).

A forty-year wait! Joshua exhibited a degree of patience that very few of us could display, regardless of age. There is much talk of the current generation of young adults being a 'Joshua generation' ready to receive the leadership of the twenty-first century church into their hands. I say just one thing – don't let's make them wait forty years. It is definitely right that young people should be groomed and developed for leadership and some will serve a long apprenticeship, but at least Joshua was by Moses' side and playing a full part in God's purposes, even whilst he was waiting to take over leadership.

David – not the obvious choice

The Lord was unhappy with Saul as king and revealed to Samuel his plans for the future: 'The LORD said to Samuel "... I am sending you to Jesse of Bethlehem. I have chosen one of his sons to be king"' (1 Sam. 16:1).

Naturally, Samuel assumed that the future king was going to be the oldest of Jesse's sons, but God had other ideas: 'When they arrived, Samuel saw Eliab and thought, "Surely the LORD's anointed stands here before the LORD.'

But the LORD said to Samuel, 'Do not consider his appearance or his height, for I have rejected him. The LORD does not look at the things man looks at. Man looks at the outward appearance, but the LORD looks at the heart' (1 Sam. 16:6,7).

It isn't always the most obvious or the oldest, or tallest, or most intelligent of the emerging generation that God calls to leadership. Perhaps the church has missed out on valuable contributions from young people because they have been seen to be too young, too inexperienced, too small, or too immature. When Samuel discovered that David was the one called to be king it was truly a landmark occasion.

God's 'one' for leadership may well not be the 'one' we would choose. For every obvious young person that a church identifies for the future, there may well be God's chosen who remains hidden. Of course, David's journey as future king wasn't an easy one. Still small and young, he struggled to be taken seriously; his brothers were angry with him when he volunteered to kill Goliath; King Saul ridiculed him for being a boy and the giant Goliath despised him. After Goliath is killed, Saul becomes jealous of David and soon wants to kill him. Jealousy, anger, and ridicule can all come the way of young people today when they struggle to be taken seriously as a part of the church, let alone when they begin to display leadership potential.

Timothy – too little experience, too young?

We discovered much about Timothy in the last chapter. One thing we did not mention was that the apostle Paul wrote two letters to Timothy to encourage him, to build him up, to keep him focused and to help him as a church leader. Here are some well-used words by everyone in youth ministry: 'Don't let anyone look down on you because you are young, but set an example for the believers in speech, in life, in love, in faith and in purity' (1 Tim. 4:12).

What we often forget when we read this verse is that at the time Timothy was probably in his late thirties or early forties! Even in the early church, some people must have found it difficult to let a younger generation play their full part in church life. Timothy had travelled with Paul and gained countless experience but that still didn't stop some folk in the church at Ephesus casting doubts about his age and experience. Paul's consistent message to Timothy was that God could use Timothy despite what anyone thought about his age, ability, confidence or experience.

Jeremiah – lacking confidence

When God first calls Jeremiah, the young prophet immediately doubted his own age and ability. Jeremiah was probably not a 'child' as the following verses state, but closer to the age of twenty

> 'Ah, Sovereign LORD,' I said, 'I do not know how to speak; I am only a child.'
>   But the LORD said to me, 'Do not say, "I am only a child." You must go to everyone I send you to and say whatever I command you. Do not be afraid of them, for I am with you and will rescue you,' declares the LORD' (Jer. 1:6-8).

God confirms to Jeremiah, that he, the Sovereign Lord, does not make mistakes and that despite Jeremiah's sense of inadequacy he will be used greatly in God's plan. To enable young people to be fully part of the church of today, we need to help them overcome their sense of inadequacy, their feeling of being overawed, and replace these feelings with a confidence in their place in the community of believers. Paul speaks to the members of the church in Corinth like this: 'Now you are the body of Christ, and each one of you is a part of it' (1 Cor. 12:27).

Young people – now!

It's revealing that in almost every translation of that verse we can read, the word 'now' is used at the start. In other words Paul is saying that our involvement in the church of Jesus isn't restricted to some time in the future when we are experienced enough or old enough. Active participation in the body of Christ is very much a 'now' thing. In fact when Jesus began to send out his followers two by two in Luke 10 he included this phrase: 'Go! I am sending you out like lambs among wolves' (verse 3). So Jesus is telling his disciples that one of the characteristics they will display is being like a 'lamb' – innocent, dependant on the shepherd, and *young*.

If your church believes the myth we are melting in this chapter then you will face the problem that I witness on a regular basis: the transition of young people from youth ministry into the adult life of the church. Even some churches with flourishing youth ministries never translate that into adult membership and 'body life' because the whole church mindset is based around an older generation and a lifestyle that is alien to young people in the twenty-first century. This is why some youth leaders opt for 'youth church' and either run a parallel young generation congregation or leave all together to form a church purely for young people.

I've got problems with youth church. For one thing, what happens when the members of youth church all reach the age of thirty or forty or fifty? In other words when does youth church finish? And for another thing, my understanding of the biblical model of church is for all backgrounds, experience, races and ages meeting together (Gal. 3:28). Now obviously, I'm completely committed to youth ministry and giving ample time to it, but I believe that that should happen in the context of the wider family of the church.

I don't blame for one minute any of you who have established a youth church, however. I'm sure you faced a brick wall in terms of the traditional church being entrenched in a time warp and making no effort to move into a greater understanding of generational church.

A youth leader says: :
'The future does depend on our young people, they are the torch-bearers. But we should be handing that torch over now.'

A youth is to be regarded with respect. How do you know his future will not be equal to our present?

Confucius

Young people locally

When we first started to advertise our Ignite Leadership Academy around Cardiff I sent an e-mail to about fifty church leaders, giving specific details about the academy being open to young people from the ages of sixteen to twenty-two. Sadly, a number of churches responded to me by saying they had nobody at all in that age group. One church in particular sent me an e-mail stating that they were surprised that we would consider anyone that young suitable for leadership, whilst another church offered a couple of people in their early forties who the church was just considering for leadership.

A few months ago I visited a church in a place called Neath near Swansea. The church is run by the pastor Wayne Carpenter, but with considerable assistance from his son and other young leaders. The church is not a youth church, but young people play an important part in every aspect of church life. As you would expect, their youth ministry is top quality, but their church is the type of place a young guy of eighteen or an old woman of seventy-five would be comfortable in. On the night I visited they had a worship band playing that consisted of people in their late teens and twenties, and then they also had two or three even younger people playing along in the band to gain experience. Wayne told me later that one or two instruments and microphones weren't actually plugged in, but nevertheless the whole set-up told me that the church took the development of and the involvement of young people seriously. They adopt the wise approach that if you really want young people to succeed you have to give them permission to fail a few times as well.

Just like Heartland Church in Fort Wayne, Bethel Elim church in Neath believe that young people are part of the church right now! One of the greatest challenges youth leaders face is to integrate young people into the life of the church, and to do that your emphasis may need to focus not on the youth ministry itself so much as the attitude of the rest of the church.

Youth would be an ideal state if it came a little later in life.

Herbert Henry Asquith

A youth worker says:
'When we say that young people have to be an important part of church life now, we aren't necessarily "dissing" the older generation!'

Young people globally

One of the most significant times in my life over recent years was when I visited the country of Haiti with a team from the child sponsorship agency Compassion. Miralda and Jean-Jacques are the names of just two people in Haiti whose stories will remain with me. Miralda is a little girl of three and a half, who has just started to receive sponsorship from Compassion. I was particularly excited to meet her, because her sponsor is my friend Lois who is one of the big fans of Esther.

Compassion workers in Haiti were able to contact the project that Miralda attended and one morning the project director brought Miralda and her mum to meet me in the Compassion offices. Miralda's mum was able to explain, with the help of an interpreter, just how pleased she was for Miralda to be sponsored: it meant that her young child was going to receive a good education, life-skills training, a school uniform and a good meal each day, as well as learning about Jesus. Already she was attending the project's kindergarten, singing gospel songs and learning communication skills such as saying 'hello', 'please' and 'thank you'. All basic stuff you think to yourself, but given Miralda's mum doesn't work, these are opportunities that otherwise would be lost to little Miralda. To meet Miralda in the very early stages of her sponsorship with Compassion went some way to showing us that the desperately poor situation that so many of Haiti's children find themselves in could be overcome.

Earlier that same morning we had heard about the *restavek* children (or 'stay with' children). Thousands of children are sent away from their rural villages by their own parents to stay with other adults in the capital Port-au-Prince, to give them a better chance at life. Unfortunately, the result is mostly the opposite – they are exploited, abused and enslaved. Compassion has been developing an afternoon strategy for the *restavek* kids, who in the mornings are press ganged into becoming sellers on the streets. Some of these children, along with the adults they live with, have already become Christians due to Compassion's practical witness.

In the evening of the same day, having seen hundreds of children's faces pressed against the car window begging for food or money, we met up with three students from Compassion Haiti's Leadership Development Programme. I sat next to Jean-Jacques, a young man nearly twenty-six years older than Miralda. He had an incredible story to tell. His parents were illiterate farmers and he didn't enter education of any sort until Compassion began to sponsor him from the age of ten. He was in two projects: one for primary education and another for secondary level. Jean-Jacques freely admits it would have been impossible for him to have even learnt to read and write but for the grace of God shown through the work of Compassion. He pays tribute to his long-time sponsor, a British pastor.

Jean-Jacques has since been selected for a university sponsorship through the Leadership Development programme, having worked part-time for Compassion as a translator to be able to afford the twenty per cent of fees he had to pay. Having finished high school at the age of twenty-three, he now works for the Salvation Army in finance, is an assistant professor at his university, and manages to pay for the education of two younger sisters. He is also the superintendent of the Sunday school in his church. As if I needed confirmation that Miralda's future had potential, here it was in the shape of Jean-Jacques.

I was blown away by the commitment of Compassion to child development and also by their commitment to give young people not just hope for the future, but an active place in the body of Christ here and now. Jean-Jacques grew up as an illiterate farmer's son but because people believed in him he is already making a significant impact in both the life of his local church and the wider body of believers.

Almost everything that is great has been done by youth.

Benjamin Disraeli

You can make a difference

When Peter addressed the assembled crowd on the day of Pentecost, one of the ways he explained what was happening was to quote from Scripture

> 'No, this is what was spoken by the prophet Joel:
> "In the last days, God says, I will pour out my Spirit on all people. Your sons and daughters will prophesy, your young men will see visions, your old men will dream dreams. Even on my servants, both men and women, I will pour out my Spirit in those days, and they will prophesy..."' (Acts 2:16-18).

Peter believed that when Joel was speaking then God was speaking, and he made reference to God's Spirit being poured out on all people – regardless of race, sex or age. All people will be party to what God wants to do and both young and old have a part to play.

If we really expect young people to be the passionate and visionary leadership of the church in the future then we must ensure that they are an active part of the body of Christ here and now. If you know that the myth of this chapter is a real problem in your church then you can do much to melt it from within:

● Keep being a good ambassador for young people and encourage them to stick with church.
● Politely but persistently question the status quo if you feel young people are being marginalized from church life.

- Encourage ways that the wider leadership could make your church more youth friendly.
- Most of all, model ways that young people can be involved in the life of the church, and constantly teach and remind the young people in your care that God's purpose for their life includes church and that means now!

✔ REALITY CHECK

1. Can you identify the barriers that your church may be putting up to the participation of young people in the life of the church right now?
2. How can you ease the transition of young people from youth ministry to church?
3. Meet with your church leaders to discuss ways of developing the church into a place where young people are central to all that goes on.
4. In Myth Five we identified the next generation of youth leaders. How can you train, equip and release them into church leadership?

MYTH 7

WE AREN'T IN THE ENTERTAINMENT BUSINESS

❝❝ Gary's Rant

Let me say right now that I believe I am in the entertainment industry!

All of us involved in youth work will know the excitement that can be generated amongst young people when the latest must-see Hollywood blockbuster is released or a favourite band is coming to town. There is a massive anticipation and when the event arrives, rarely are young people let down because the producers generally know what to create in order to stimulate all the senses. Contrast this with what most young people expect from church. Is there the same buzz and excitement? In most cases there is not, largely because we use outdated models.

When preaching really came into its own during the Age of Enlightenment, the church did not have the monopoly on public speakers. In fact an increasingly popular form of entertainment was going to listen to a public lecture where a man (for it was almost without exception a man) would talk at people for up to two hours. In those days the church was leading popular culture and not ignoring it.

Over the last few years I have had the privilege to work with some amazing entertainers, all of them Christians. As a result of these entertainers using their God-given gifts, I have been able to see thousands come to faith and even more young people fired with a passion to be radical disciples. Artists like DC Talk, Rebecca St James, Newsboys, Superhero, Delirious? and The Tribe all strive to bring an excellent show to their audience so that they can build a bridge into popular culture in order that the gospel might be heard. Are they in the entertainment business? Yes they are! Their credibility as carriers of good news is built on their ability to engage and hold an increasingly sophisticated and discerning audience. To do this they employ the best sound and lighting systems and work very hard on their stage show and all aspects of the production.

Occasionally a criticism will be aimed at artists along the lines of 'they are only entertaining, just fun with no substance.' In some cases this is true but I think that can be acceptable. Perhaps we should sometimes do things in our youth ministry just for fun (of course, sometimes despite our best efforts, they are not entertaining!) Our sense of disappointment with the band that did not proclaim Jesus loud enough is sometimes because we have been guilty of investing too much in them to do our job.

> You might say we do not have the budget of Hollywood or the big record companies. This is true but neither do they have the most powerful resource. We have the Holy Spirit.

This generation is entertaining itself to death.

Chris Cole, Cross Rhythms Festival 2003

Are we entertainers? Do we entertain?

The following thoughts are from an American youth pastor who has grave reservations about using the term 'entertainment'. He worries that he may be building his ministry on light-hearted amusement whilst the really important stuff might be seen to be boring. His concerns not only reflect one area of concern about this myth, but also reflect a kick-back against the 'entertainment at all costs' culture of some youth groups

The kids I work with – they're good at finding joy in entertainment, but what about worship? Or prayer? Or reading the Bible? Personally, I think worship is piles of fun. I find joy in it. But that kid sitting on the couch over there doesn't. He's bored silly, poor guy. Somehow I have to teach him to find joy in the things that matter most. But is what I'm saying lining up with what I'm doing? On one hand I tell him that he doesn't need alcohol (a frivolous diversion) to have fun, but I've been peppering our youth events with frivolous diversions of other kinds for years now.

Brad Huebert, 'Musing about Amusement', *Youthworker*, July/August 2003[i]

This is possibly the most complex of the myths to melt, with many strong voices on both sides of the discussion. How we define the words 'entertainment' and 'business' will have a large bearing on our conclusions. I actually believe that many of us have a real problem with the word 'entertainment' because of all the modern baggage attached to it: it has become sordid, sleazy, frivolous and lightweight. The dictionary definition does little to dispel this myth.

Entertainment is:
● The various ways of amusing people, especially by performing for them.
● The amount of pleasure or amusement you get from something.
● Something that is produced or performed for an audience.

Reading those definitions we'd all agree that youth ministry is so much more than this, and that we've really short-changed what we do if we simply think it is entertainment.

Buzz words such as 'infotainment', 'infomercials', and 'edutainment' can be found in the world of marketing and publicity. They more or less all mean the same thing: getting an important message across but in an entertaining and memorable way – a cross between the commercial and informative, a blend of education and entertainment. I don't want to overstate this case, but some youth leaders would do well to adopt that approach. For some that will mean a little more entertainment and a little less information and for others it will mean a little less entertainment and a bit more education. Ultimately, of course, the church is all about transformation, but memorable and enjoyable spiritual experiences go a long way to help transform a young person from a lost soul into a disciple of Jesus.

'Do not forget to entertain strangers, for by so doing some people have entertained angels without knowing it' (Heb. 13:2).

A youth leader says:
**'If we aren't entertaining young people then just
look at the alternative entertainment on offer!'**

Let's turn our attention to the word 'entertain'. Here's what the dictionary says.

To entertain:
- Engage a person or audience by providing amusing or interesting material.
- To offer hospitality, especially in your home.
- To turn something over in your mind.

Now that's more like it. I guess we would all want to entertain if it means engaging young people with interesting material, offering hospitality and reflecting over what we do and how we do it. Don't we want young people to be welcomed, engaged and urged to reflect?

Jesus the entertainer

Without detracting one bit from his holiness, his saving work on the cross and his deity, I want to state that Jesus knew what it meant to entertain and to be entertained. He welcomed the opportunity to be offered hospitality in the homes of Martha, Levi and Zacchaeus. He had large crowds amazed and astonished at his words and feats. Matthew tells us, 'When Jesus had finished saying these things, the crowds were amazed at his teaching' and 'When the crowds heard this they were astonished at his teaching' (Mt. 7:28; 22:33).

Jesus knew the power of an entertaining story. Just imagine the faces of the disciples as he was telling an expert in the law the parable of the Good Samaritan, or the faces of the crowd when he was telling the parable of the sower. Imagine the scene at the Sermon on the Mount!

Jesus was a visual communicator too – his stories evoked clear pictures for listeners to envisage. Fields white and ready for harvest, a lamp burning under a bed or hidden in a jar, flocks of sheep and goats, a tiny coin hidden in a house, a man digging up a field.

In fact, Jesus didn't just talk visually but he acted visually as well. Consider the visual impact of spitting in your hands, making some mud, spreading it on a blind man's eyes and giving him his sight back. Consider the impact of bending down in front of the teachers of the law and a condemned woman and drawing pictures in the sand. Imagine the wide-eyed amazement of his followers when Jesus walked on water, or when he calmed the storm. So important was 'story' as a communication tool for Jesus that Mark's gospel makes a special mention of it: 'How can we picture God's kingdom? What kind of story can we use? ... With many stories like these, he presented his message to them, fitting the stories to their experience and maturity. He was never without a story when he spoke' (Mk. 4:30,33, *The Message*).

Jesus entertained, but his main audience was the hearts of the people he spoke to. Humour was in his repertoire too. The rich young ruler has had an enlightening encounter with Jesus but departs with sadness because he isn't prepared to readjust his priorities: 'When he heard this, he became very sad, because he was a man of great wealth. Jesus looked at him and said, "How hard it is for the rich to enter the kingdom of God! Indeed, it is easier for a camel to go through the eye of a needle than for a rich man to enter the kingdom of God"' (Lk. 18:23-25).

At first glance, Jesus' comments to the disciples as he sees the man leave, paint a ridiculous enough picture of a camel trying to get through the eye of a needle. Bible scholars tell us that a small gate into the walled city of Jerusalem was given the nickname 'eye of the needle' and so Jesus is evoking a familiar image of traders vainly

attempting to squeeze their camel through that small gate.
Even in the disappointment of the rich man's departure,
Jesus is able to use a word picture that would cause an
amused bewilderment on the face of the disciples.

A youth leader says:
**'It should be illegal to present the gospel in a
boring way.'**

Are we in a business?

Both Gary and I straddle the world of youth ministry and the
Christian music industry. It's not always easy to have a foot
in both camps, and well-respected veterans of the Christian
music scene such as Steve Taylor have grave reservations
about the arena of influence they once inhabited

> *I've got nothing against Christian entertainment, and I
> certainly support excellence in worship music and other
> forms of artistic expression being produced for the church. I
> just think we've got more than enough. Meanwhile, we've
> seen an unprecedented rise in mainstream entertainment
> targeted at kids that steals their innocence and rapes their
> minds. And what did we expect? The Bible says we reap
> what we sow. We've sowed virtually nothing in that world.
> We've spent all our efforts and resources in building a
> Christian entertainment subculture. And guess what? It's
> now so profitable that most of it's been purchased by some
> of the same mainstream media conglomerates that exist
> solely to increase shareholder value.*

> **Steve Taylor, 'Are You a Minister or an Entertainer?',**
> **Youthspecialties.com, December 2002**[ii]

In his opening rant, Gary mentioned his work with a
variety of Christian bands and artists. He handles all the
UK and European concert booking and touring for Rebecca

St James for example. I spend three or four weeks a year travelling on the road in the United States with the band Third Day as their 'road pastor' and used to do the same with the Newsboys. Gary and I firmly believe in Christian music as a tool for evangelism and for discipleship, and we seek to use it strategically in Ignite whenever we can. Yet both of us do share some of the same reservations as Steve Taylor, and perhaps even more about the suitability of putting the words 'Christian music' and 'industry' together. We would be devastated to see youth ministry become a business, and even now recognize that a rapidly growing area of business is the area of youth ministry resources.

Again, however, if we look to the dictionary for some guidance then two of the possible definitions of 'business' are as follows:

● Personal responsibilities and concerns
● Tasks or important things

So I'm happy to define all I do under the calling of God as 'business' in those terms, and especially can see that youth ministry could justifiably be called our business.

One of my responsibilities with Newsboys was to organize a youth leaders' reception before the start of every concert. Phil Joel from the band used to pop in and thank the youth leaders for coming along. Phil would say 'we do the same job as you guys, except we do it louder!' The attitude of the rest of the band was the same in that they all believed they were ministering to young people through the medium of music *and* by being entertainers.

Now we shouldn't just define entertainment as music, and the complex scenario of the Christian music industry is best left for another book, but it does suggest that it can be possible to reconcile the role of 'minister' with that of 'entertainer'. In fact I would say that entertainment can add much to ministry, providing it never becomes the major focus.

Don't cultivate a consumer culture

One of the problems of the Christian entertainment scene is that it can make consumers out of all of us. Our yearly programme is liberally sprinkled with trips to our favourite events, to the popular bands, listening to the cool worship leaders and following the big name speakers. Unless we are very careful this breeds a type of Christianity which is all about 'what's in it for me' rather than a self-sacrificing lifestyle of discipleship. Ignite first sprang up in Cardiff as a response to a crowd of half-hearted teenagers from churches across the city, who turned up at events just to please themselves, and picked and chose Christian activities as if they were choosing what TV programme to watch or what magazine to buy. We have tried to instil a culture where entertainment isn't of paramount importance: meeting with God and serving him are the key factors. What is important is that these can be achieved in an entertaining way. If the young people in your youth group are only around to be amused and entertained without recognizing anything deeper then you have work to do!

A youth leader says:
'Don't forget that style isn't everything.'

Don't let the media become the message

As far as possible I'm committed to using live music, video clips, powerpoint and a variety of other 'entertainment' to communicate Jesus into the lives of young people. I don't for a minute suggest that youth ministry is simply about offering young people lightweight and sanitised alternatives to mainstream entertainment, and I despair of youth ministry that is so crammed with silly games, loud videos, computers fun trips, and purely social stuff that there is never any room for real discipleship. I've been in plenty of meetings too, when a powerful message has been sacrificed on the altar of a trendy video clip or culturally relevant watered-down illustrations.

Yet young people do want to be entertained and youth ministry is competing with a high-tech age of entertainment; so it must be full of attractive, memorable and entertaining moments. In the best sense of the word we recognize that Jesus was an entertainer. He used story, parable, humour and had a unique ability to entertain large crowds. Just as we aim to 'entertain' guests properly in our homes, so we must aim to 'entertain' guests in the house of God. The counterbalance to this recognizes that youth ministry cannot simply be about a lightweight, glitzy, entertaining style that contains no substance.

As we look at the example of Jesus we see that his attractive and entertaining style always contained a powerful and sometimes difficult message. Youth ministry must always be relevant, and must communicate in ways that connect with young people, but must never do this to the extent that the message of Jesus is compromised. The centrality of Jesus, the love of God and the presence of the Holy Spirit must always be paramount. The Bible reminds us that the foolishness of the cross is our focal point (1 Cor. 1:18), and we should never let the method overtake the message, or the media detract from the incredible good news that we proclaim.

I came to you in weakness and fear, and with much trembling. My message and my preaching were not with wise and persuasive words, but with a demonstration of the Spirit's power, so that your faith might not rest on men's wisdom, but on God's power (1 Cor. 2:3-5).

✔ REALITY CHECK

1. Have you struck the right balance between entertainer and minister?
2. What do you think takes priority in your youth ministry – style or content?
3. How can you more effectively entertain young people in the church?
4. Do you attempt to entertain too much? How can you readjust?

Notes

i Originally published in *Youthworker*, copyright 2004, Salem Publishing/CCM Communications. Reprinted with permission. For subscription information, visit www.youthworker.com

ii Originally published in *Youthworker*, copyright 2004. Reprinted with permission.

CONCLUSION: TRUTH OR MYTH?

So there are the seven myths that we've identified and melted down for you. In their place we've attempted to place Biblical truth and an element of common sense! Inevitably, some of what we have shared has been 'our opinion' or 'what we think'. However rooted in scripture and eloquently expressed, there has still been an element of opinion, experience and thinking from Gary and myself. So here's the challenge for you: don't just take our word for it, but go back to the Bible and work through these myths for yourself. Truth is mentioned in the Bible two hundred and fourteen times – so it's high on the agenda! You will never hear Jesus say 'in my opinion' or 'I think' or 'in my experience', but in the gospels he uses the phrase 'I tell you the truth' – on seventy-eight instances. Jesus will always be your ultimate source of truth – about yourself, about life, about these myths. This book has aimed to follow that principle, but you should double-check it.

The postmodern world that we live in tries to tell us that there is no such thing as absolute truth, or an absolute objective point of view in areas of morality and religion. We need to guard ourselves against this attitude infiltrating the foundational truths on which we build our youth ministry. We can't afford to be people who take the attitude that says:

'You have your truth and I have mine' or that says 'Don't confuse us with the facts'.

If we allow myth, misguided thinking or guiding parameters that are based on anything but scripture, to govern the way we express our ministry then we are simply like that foolish man who built his house on sand rather than the one who built on rock.

The whole of the Ignite initiative enables young people to build on a solid foundation for a life of following Jesus, and encourages youth leaders to build from a solid platform too.

You might want to check the youth leader page on our web site www.igniteme.org it often has some useful teaching material and resources.

Whether we are talking about your whole life, your youth ministry, or even an individual project, you always have the two choices that Jesus speaks of in Matthew 7 (NLT):

It will fall with a mighty crash.

Or

It won't collapse, because it is built on rock.

A person of truth will always be a powerful instrument in God's hands. Some people will be angry with you when you question things, others will resent you for showing honesty and integrity, others will want you to jump on board the latest trend, but providing you always seek the truth in what you do, and are always willing to measure the prevailing thinking against God's truth, then you will be used powerfully.

Keep melting those myths and keep igniting a passion for Jesus!

THE MAGNIFICENT SEVEN

Here are seven short statements that summarise how to melt each myth we've been examining:

Give all the time you can to young people

Aim for growth in quality and quantity

Commit to effective, contemporary and Biblical preaching

Seek vision from God and follow it

Build commitment into the life of young people

Integrate young people into the life of the church

Engage and entertain young people in God's house

If you have any comments about any of the myths or you have discovered some myths that we haven't mentioned then please email us:

Nigel@igniteme.org
Gary@igniteme.org